WITNESSING PERFECTION

First published by O Books, 2008
O Books is an imprint of John Hunt Publishing Ltd., The Bothy, Deershot Lodge, Park Lane, Ropley,
Hants, SO24 0BE, UK
office1@o-books.net
www.o-books.net

Distribution in:	South Africa
	Alternative Books
UK and Europe	altbook@peterhyde.co.za
Orca Book Services	Tel: 021 555 4027 Fax: 021 447 1430
orders@orcabookservices.co.uk	
Tel: 01202 665432 Fax: 01202 666219	Text copyright Shaykh Fadhlalla Haeri 2008
Int. code (44)	
	Design: Stuart Davies
USA and Canada	
NBN	ISBN: 978 1 84694 142 9
custserv@nbnbooks.com	
Tel: 1 800 462 6420 Fax: 1 800 338 4550	All rights reserved. Except for brief quotations
	in critical articles or reviews, no part of this
Australia and New Zealand	book may be reproduced in any manner without
Brumby Books	prior written permission from the publishers.
sales@brumbybooks.com.au	
Tel: 61 3 9761 5535 Fax: 61 3 9761 7095	The rights of Shaykh Fadhlalla Haeri as author
	have been asserted in accordance with the
Far East (offices in Singapore, Thailand,	Copyright, Designs and Patents Act 1988.
Hong Kong, Taiwan)	
Pansing Distribution Pte Ltd	
kemal@pansing.com	A CIP catalogue record for this book is available
Tel: 65 6319 9939 Fax: 65 6462 5761	from the British Library.

Copyright Zahra Trust UK

Printed and Bound by Digital Book Print Ltd
www.digitalbookprint.com

O Books operates a distinctive and ethical publishing philosophy in
all areas of its business, from its global network of authors to
production and worldwide distribution.
This book is produced on FSC certified stock, within ISO14001
standards. The printer plants sufficient trees each year through
the Woodland Trust to absorb the level of emitted carbon in
its production.

WITNESSING
PERFECTION

Shaykh Fadhlalla Haeri

BOOKS

Winchester, UK
Washington, USA

CONTENTS

PREFACE

To acquire any knowledge one needs serious intention, proper tutelage and application. For spiritual knowledge one needs to go beyond the mind, intellect and the limitation of thoughts and space-time habits. Then the light of inspiration from the inner heart will radiate. One of the meanings of "the meek shall inherit the earth" is that a genuine state of being inwardly bereft, desperate and humble are prerequisites for openings, insights and spiritual awakening to truth and absolute justice.

Reliable spiritual evolvement starts with the discovery that creation appears as duality and the balance of opposites, whose roots are the one cosmic source and essence of all life. Dualities and diversities of experiences are based on an all-embracing unity, which encompasses the entire macrocosm as well as all the microcosms. Human biological evolution seems to have been accompanied by growth in consciousness and spiritual evolution. Consciousness is based upon awareness and self identity and concern and the quest for joy and happiness.

Human experiences encompasses two complementary streams of consciousness, one of which is personal, conditioned, evolving and developing, whilst the other is constant (pure or high consciousness) and not subject to movement and change. Enlightenment entails the unity of these consciousnesses and their harmony and balance. The perplexing question of deity and purpose of life can only be satisfactorily answered through the lens of unity, so that all that is experienced is properly understood by reference to higher consciousness and the one essence from which everything has emanated and is energized. Durable contentment is a result of this perfected vision and multi focused state.

In classical times higher education covered logic, aesthetics, ethics, politics as well as metaphysics. In our present day due to the supremacy of a scientific and technologically driven way of life we need to bring back the study of metaphysics and knowledges via the humanly accessible supreme consciousness. This will enable us to fill the missing gap in our understanding of cosmic unity and creational diversity and inseparability of the absolute and relative. Ancient cultures have rich oral traditions of myths and tales which connected life on earth to beyond space-time limitations.

Every human being is composed of an eternal soul reflecting pure consciousness and its companion self, with its evolving but limited consciousness. Each self is driven by the power of love to discover the divine attributes already etched within the soul. Acts of worship, prayer and faith are the expressions of human desires and adoration of god's perfect qualities or virtues. Vices are the dark side of virtues. God's eternal light and its presence within the human soul is the constant guide and reference point of the self evolving towards unification with its soul and attaining its fulfilment. One of the meanings of the fall of Adam and Eve from paradise is that of the rise of dual consciousness. In paradise there was only pure consciousness and once self identity (eating from the tree of duality – cause and effect) occurred then there is the need to rise again to unify with the original and ever present supreme consciousness.

I grew up to regard Sufism and Islam as clear summations of the Abrahamic prophetic revelations for spiritual transformation. Understanding the closeness between the essences of Christianity, Judaism, Islam and other religions became clearer to me by looking at these traditions through the unifying light of the one all encompassing consciousness. This vision is accessible at all times and by all people, irrespective of culture or religion, when the self and soul are united within the purified heart.

This book emerges from the fertile Islamic Sufi gnostic garden of knowledge and light. It is based upon the foundation that there is only one true reality that is both within as well as beyond all spatial and temporal entities. This omnipotent and omnipresent reality or god is the power behind all human desires to know the purpose of life and live contentedly. The purpose of a true religion is to guide towards this goal.

During the last forty years of my life, I have lived in eight different countries for lengthy durations of time. This entailed relating to different cultures, values and languages. I have studied, taught and worked in different commercial fields; managing (not without struggle) to reconcile a well defined eastern culture and religious background with the amorphous prevailing world order. The altar of worship in the first world is personal achievement and success. Its emphasis on self interest and material success above all else seemed to me an indicator of spiritual malaise.

The globalisation of commerce, technology and information means that the old ways of moral and ethical living and account-ability to family and community are not easy to apply any more. An urgent re-balance between head and heart is needed. This can only be fulfilled by personal spiritual evolvement, personal commitment and connections with like-minded and like-hearted others, through the new global communication networks, which can compensate to some degree for physical distance and dispersion. Every age has its difficulties as well as its solutions but human beings can survive and grow in this world by assuming the responsible role of stewardship with full account-ability for the welfare of the whole earth.

In this book I hope to share with the reader ways to live actively and responsibly, cheerfully and lightheartedly. We have no choice other than to aim at outer excellence whilst attempting to witness perfection with our spiritual lens at all times, irrespective of personalised views of each situation. Wherever there is a shadow there is also light that has caused it and the entire universe is contained within the eternal cosmic light. It is the light of light that will transform us to our spiritual reality beyond the personal and worldly limitations of cause and effect and all the constants of space-time.

INTRODUCTION

Lasting fulfilment can only be achieved when an aspect of perfection is perceived within every moment. Every moment contains a glimpse of perfection. The rational mind relates to the world of cause and effect and guides us to physical survival and well-being. The heart and soul is what distinguishes humanity and enables us to relate to the unseen worlds beyond time and space. This earth is the nursery where every creation evolves to the highest level of its consciousness within its capacity.

The mind and senses connect the individual self with the outer world, whereas the heart connects the self with the soul and the subtler worlds. The source of all created souls is a unique cosmic essence, which we have named God, which energizes diverse entities and beings. Every soul carries within it attributes that reflect aspects of this cosmic soul. The human soul potentially knows and desires numerous aspects of this essence such as life, power, knowledge, beauty, majesty and many more besides. The soul of the ant is restricted to only a few patterns of behaviour such as survival, protection, feeding, procreation and other basic evolutionary programmes. Every soul is designed and packaged to carry out efficiently its role in life as part of the universal interplay of dualities and creational possibilities, all within an interconnected cosmic unity.

The light of the supreme divine soul permeates and envelops every aspect of creation. It is at the root of life, death, under-standing, ignorance, good, bad, the seen, the unseen, acceptance, rejection, contentment, discontentment, order, chaos, light, darkness, awareness and consciousness. The human soul is imprinted with this truth and it beams this energy towards the specific self. This relationship is the root of the belief that the human soul knows its lord and the divine qualities, carrying a special responsibility and privilege on earth. Personal consciousness arises from soul consciousness and these two energy streams constitute the unique human state which seeks higher knowledge into realms beyond worldly limitations.

Life is experienced through movement and change. Everything in this world is relative within time and space, yet we always seek constancy of what is desirable and elimination of what is undesirable. We prefer lasting health to short bursts of super wellness. We look for lasting safety, security, love, contentment and stability. In fact, the human desire for perpetuity and immortality is a direct reflection of the attribute of the eternally perfect soul within our heart.

As the body and mind grow and identify with each other there arises the personal awareness of self consciousness with the idea of individuality, separation and independence. This self consciousness can be the cause of much human confusion and suffering, as well as of natural evolvement, harmony and unity with the soul. The self with its mind and reasoning links the mineral, vegetative and animal levels within the human being efficiently and instinctively. The soul is like a divine hologram containing and reflecting all the higher qualities and attributes, which the self admires and loves. A holographic image usually depicts a visible entity, but in this case the example of the hologram is used in a qualitative sense. When the self (and ego) is in alignment with the soul, it experiences harmony and contentment; otherwise it is restless, confused and demanding. Thus, the question of the meaning and purpose of life and psychological wellbeing rests upon the unison between self and soul consciousness, which can take place when the inner heart is purified and receptive.

To understand the nature of creation, we need to reflect upon the intricate connections and relation between dualities, the dynamics of cause and effect, the differences between the subtle and gross, meaning and form, inner and outer worlds, the permanent and transitory and what is within space-time and what is beyond.

In our present time, the prevailing global human trend is biased towards material and physical pursuits. This state needs to be balanced by greater concern for the human soul, the psyche and the intricate relationship between body, mind, ego, heart and soul. There are always a few individuals who concentrate on spiritual unfoldment but it is also not unusual for people who have suffered worldly disappointments or failures to seriously search for purpose and meaning in life. Every human being at sometime or another has questioned their purpose and direction in life and has desired to know what brings about lasting contentment. Ultimately real 'fulfilment' is the outcome of the unison between heart and head or soul and self.

To achieve this unison or harmony the challenge for all spiritual seekers is the constant need to act appropriately at every moment, aiming for excellence in intention and action. To do the right thing in the right way, at the right time and place, is the foundation of quality living. Freedom from confusing choices and habitual mistakes will gradually increase with heightened self awareness and continual reference to higher wisdom.

Human endeavours and desires are balanced between attraction towards that which brings ease and contentment and repulsion from difficulty and confusion. To transcend the battle of dualities we need to refer to a higher consciousness and truth. The first station in this journey is factual awareness of outer events and one's inner state. Then a clear rational mind and intellect can lead to reflection from the heart and soul and thus light and guidance. This process of combining rationality with spontaneous and intuitive insight comes about when head and heart are in unison and consciousness is unified.

In our present world mathematics, physics and most other sciences are the same for everyone, anywhere, in every culture. Ethics, however, have not yet fully evolved into a universally acceptable code of conduct by diverse cultures and religions; this can only happen when we acknowledge and experience pure consciousness and tap into absolute truth. From this higher knowledge different levels of ethical boundaries and acceptable human conduct will emerge. It is unethical to steal but if it was the last resort for survival, then most people would forgive this 'wrong' conduct. Thus there is a hierarchy of understandable behaviour based upon seeking the universally desirable state of survival wellness and contentment whilst interacting with the world of uncertainties.

This is a personal book about spiritual philosophy and is condensed within seven chapters, covering a range of issues concerning creation, realities, truth, the different dimensions of the self, levels of consciousness, perceptions, relationships and the meaning and state of inner enlightenment. God, supreme consciousness or divine light, is the thread that runs throughout the book. Chapter one describes the foundation of existence and creation. Chapter two deals with the human template and the cosmic unity behind all diversity. Chapter three describes the growth and evolvement of the human self through its journey to the wisdom and serenity of the soul within its heart. Chapter four describes the different levels of relationships in creation and their interplay. Chapter five addresses the human purpose and meaning in life and personal salvation. Chapter six discusses the root of the human quest and desire for security and lasting perfection. Chapter seven presents summaries, prescriptions and descriptions of the fulfilled self.

This book requires the reader's serious involvement and deep interaction for it to yield the intended benefit of transformation. Please pay attention to the words and terms used in this text, as they differ from other popular versions. I have tried to avoid unnecessary religious, spiritual or philosophical language for simplicity and clarity. The lack of capitalisation is a deliberate act to reduce our pre-conditioned prejudices for names and concepts. Open the book at any place and you will gain some wisdom and insight according to your readiness and the level of your freedom from mindsets and other cultural limitations and habits.

The major theme which is woven throughout this book is that two different domains — space-time and beyond — meet within the human heart. The convergence of the relative and absolute worlds can generate confusion as well as reliable guidance within us. These two worlds have different cosmologies and logic, and need to be distinguished with every move. The first domain is the outer world of time and space: this requires rationality, a clear head, the reasoning and wisdom of causality and context, appropriate skills, training, discipline and goals. The other domain is the inner, unseen spiritual world whose supra-logic relates to soul and heart, pure consciousness and joy. These two worlds meet within every human being: they need to be acknowledged and unified. Success in the outer world needs ambition and drive whereas the spiritual world needs submission and abandonment to the soul within or the supreme consciousness and cosmic essence.

To fully benefit and be transformed by this book you need to read, reflect and apply what touches and benefits you most. This process should be repeated until you gain spontaneous access to your inner heart by blocking mental interference. Apply what is relevant to you at the time and trust that there is perfection within every situation and experience. We experience time and space through the mind and conditioned self, which has been empowered by its partner, the soul. Personal and conditioned consciousness is energised by soul consciousness. Unison between personal and soul consciousness will open the door to witnessing perfection along the whole spectrum of consciousness.

The journey of the spiritual seeker begins by looking for meaning and patterns behind events, feelings and experiences. The compass of this journey is the reference to the essence of life, which is the soul within the human's heart. When all dualities and opposites are seen through this unified lens, all of these experiences and events will change in meaning and significance. Conflicts, difficulties and disappointments will no longer bring about undue suffering and emotional reactions. This new state of authentic understanding enables the person to interact wisely with the outer world, whilst experiencing harmony and ease at heart. The door to the magnificent present moment and the joy therein begins to open.

When you begin to see the perfection within different events and experiences, irrespective of personal and cultural judgement, you are at the shores of the divine ocean of bliss. Your heart is now the altar of your worship and your soul is the source of lasting security and joy. This state of awakening combines worldly rationality and wisdom with spontaneous spiritual light and perfect presence.

All human beings desire to experience perfection and goodness each moment. We constantly struggle to transcend the changing world of dualities and opposites to the tranquillity of peace and constancy. The perfect presence reveals itself when all dualities have been submerged in the light of unity.

This book is about how people can transform their understanding and perception to witness reality through the lens of pure consciousness. This new atunement does not deny personal experiences, preferences or emotions, but by looking at them through the inner lens one realises how insignificant most of one's mental values are. Even an inkling of this possibility and understanding will reduce the impact of life's stresses and produce spiritual hope and progress.

Most authentic spiritual paths show how to navigate in life by concentrating upon 'how', whilst postponing the 'why' questions. This concern over why fades away and becomes redundant in the light of self realisation and transformation due to awakened joyfulness. This state of living in contentment is due to the unity of consciousness reflecting the unity of god, the essence of life and the supreme cosmic consciousness.

Much of this book is easy to follow but there are parts which require careful reading through a spiritual lens, otherwise they will not be understood and could be misleading. Even the book's main theme of 'witnessing perfection' has to be put into perspective. It is undeniable that on a day-to-day basis we struggle to bring about balance and harmony in our apparently imperfect lives. Yet it is only by stepping out of one's self that the impartial, illumined heart is able to experience perfection in all circumstances beyond the changing good and bad. The aphorisms interwoven throughout the text are points for contemplation and deeper reflection; they help the reader to look again with a new focus and deeper insight.

I request the reader to approach this book with an open mind and heart and resonate with it wherever possible. Let it 'take you', rather than you 'get it'. It is like a tapestry with patterns and colours appearing in clusters and patches, making it a living flying carpet. Accept the recurring designs and colours for they are part of the multi-dimensional design of this prayer mat. As you read, leave aside your analytical or critical mind and participate with the author in living the process of transmitting the text and absorbing it. We human beings are all like the changing shadows, illumined by the one eternal light whose spark shines in every heart. We need to allow that natural process to lead us.

Your sickness is from you – but you do not perceive it,
Your remedy is within you – but you do not sense it,
You presume that you are a small entity – whereas within you is
*   enfolded the entire universe.*
You are indeed the evident book, by whose alphabet the hidden
*   becomes manifest*
Therefore you have no need to look beyond yourself; what you seek
*   is within you, if only you reflect.*

(Imam Ali Ibn Abi Talib)

1. CREATIONAL DYNAMICS

Every entity in creation is considered alive, sentient or conscious when it exhibits an identity whose energy source is light or other subtler powers such as radiation, electromagnetism or even less detectable energies.

Rain began to fall a few billion years ago and for centuries it never stopped. The vast oceans and barren rocks continued the long process of upheaval and massive change. After many millions of years the cosmic rays connected the atoms of carbon and hydrogen, giving birth to the primordial cell and the spark of life. Several million years later, tiny sticky gel droplets began to develop membranes, leading eventually to the emergence of the protein molecule. The identity of a living being was seeded, the cosmic ray acting as father and mother, the primeval sea of primitive flotsam of living cells being the womb. After a few hundred million years, multi-cellular life began and the semi-permeable membrane veiled the mysteries of the cosmic enactment within the cell. The urge for survival, growth and procreation was rooted in the divided cell, from its early separation, as distinct from its cosmic parentage. Thus, our evolving world emerged from non-existence by the empowerment of a boundless cosmic essence and light which created countless species and entities with different levels of consciousness creeping along the path of natural and survival of the fittest. Then came another wave of consciousness which produced self awareness, dualities, separation and gatheredness, space-time and ideas leading to speculation about what lies beyond the limitations of body and mind. This is the event of the human quest to discover the one essence or source behind all diverse and different entities. Energy and matter are ever bound to each other, interacting and reflecting the connections between all tangible and non-material entities in the heavens and on earth. The human being's unique position in this world is due to self-awareness, identity and the complementary links in consciousness between body, mind, intellect, heart and soul. The human psyche is the meeting point of what is seen and the unseen. The universe is like a vast ocean and each person is like a little boat in need of direction and efficient steering. To arrive at the intended destiny along the shore of our origin, we need awareness of the outer situation, whilst coordinating and unifying the skipper, the ocean and the boat.

All worldly experiences occur in relation to numerous opposites, which originate from one eternal essence or source that is also present and acts within space-time. This essence, where all relative and transitory events are connected and unified, is the cause of the human drive towards meaning and purpose in life. It is also what brings about lasting harmony between mind and heart and awareness of such progress. The ultimate human quest for permanent happiness can only be attained by witnessing the eternal perfection emanating from this essence, which contains all the divine qualities of beauty, majesty, love, generosity and other desirable attributes, which permeate creation. Vices and difficulties are also part of the creational designs of shadows guiding us towards the light behind them. A disappointment is simply the dark side of the 'appointment'. The physical world is a theatre where all possible tangible manifestations and subtle realities – qualitative and quantitative, seen and unseen – exist and interact. Other worlds are illuminated and permeated by the same one divine unique light of lights, giving rise to consciousness, discernment and infinite varieties of forms and energy waves. Human beings have the potential awareness of awakening to this higher consciousness by connecting and reconciling the self/mind with soul consciousness, by means of the purified heart.

During the billions of years in which countless diverse and complex creations were evolving, the unifying essence remained unknown until the advent of the human consciousness. Our spectrum of consciousness contains the originating impulse, which existed before the first flicker of life within the cell. We experience life from its inception and in all its associated forms and manifestations. Within the inner folds of the human heart and soul lies the design of whatever occurred over the course of billions of years yet is still happening now. Therein lies the meeting point between the supreme source of creation and all that exists emanates from it and depends upon its perfection. The human paradox and mystery is due to the inexplicable connection within our soul of two complementary realms with different foundations, one being worldly and subject to space-time, the other beyond it yet operating within it – not unlike the quantum world of physics.

Existence contains every conceivable and imaginable creation, every combination of form and energy. Everything that exists connects and relates to everything else within space-time and beyond.

1.1. WEB OF LIFE

All the diverse life forms we see today have arisen and evolved naturally from the distant past along the pattern of the tree of life.

Our world is comprised of innumerable simple and complex systems, delicate and structured domains and ecosystems inhabited by countless definable as well as intangible energies and entities. These creations all interact and influence each other via numerous networks of channels and fields of forces and energies. This world of appearances and energy streams constantly interact at physical, chemical, electromagnetic and other levels. Every substance is characterised by colour, shape, size, smell, taste and other discernable qualities and sensory distinctions. Every molecule vibrates at a frequency according to its density and atomic structure. Every entity broadcasts its natural characteristics whose code and language can only be understood by other creations connected to its sphere of life and influence. The web of life contains worlds within worlds relating to other worlds of wider dimensions and durations.

Every created entity follows its innate programme, manifests its state and returns to its basic origin, which is already encoded within it.

Our discernible earthly macrocosmic world is reproduced and complemented by countless microcosmic worlds, which include dark matters, plasmas and numerous other unknown forces and energy fields. All of these domains are held together within a space-time web by a unique essence whose domain extends beyond our perception and imagination. This most subtle unifying power permeates heavens and earth and is called god, supreme consciousness, or truth. This zone of absolute perfection leads to other levels of the relative absolute where qualities of complementarities appear as refractions of the original essence. Then there are the spheres of creational patterns and 'archetypes', followed by the world of discernable dominions and materials. All diverse entities in our physical world remain connected to the original pure essence through countless souls at different levels of sentiency, consciousness and limitations.

God is the light of lights and the source of all conditioned and modified lights in heaven and earth. Everything in existence has its root in this supreme essence and aspires to its perfection according to its soul's ability.

Everything in existence is in constant flux. Today is the child of yesterday and the mother of tomorrow. The world is crisscrossed by highways and strings of interchanging energies and vibrations, creating the illusion of a stable and continuous reality. Living cells are bounded by semi-permeable membranes and as such constantly interact with their surrounding environment, yet every cell maintains an individual identity and dynamic stability. The evolution of the human self from a single cell to a full complex being mirrors the evolution of life on earth. The moment of conception echoes the cosmic big bang. Both of these events signify the human birth, dispersion (as a baby grows independent of its parents), eventual disintegration and death. Yet the soul's ongoingness reflects god's eternal nature and drives the human search for knowledge and discovery.

The divine light gives rise to cosmic consciousness which manifests as a spectrum with multiple dimensions. The human being contains dual consciousnesses – the personal conditioned and short-lived as well as on-going soul consciousness.

It is through movement and change that the human self (through the mind) is motivated to seek satisfaction of needs or wants in order to attain stability and contentment. Life is experienced as a constant quest for balance and harmony within ever-changing conditions, polarities and dualities. The self is faced with structured confinement within space-time, whilst its source of life is the soul, which is eternal and free from all earthly or physical constraints.

There are as many ways to god as there are human beings or creations. In truth there is only god and everything else emanates as grace or mercy.

Love is the primal divine power permeating all of creation and holding the universe in dynamic balance. Love is the root cause for all actions, desires, connections, relationships, dispersions and unifications. Love is the drive for knowledge, freedom, contentment and joy. When love becomes directed towards another person or entity it becomes restricted and limited. It is this original primal love which propels us to seek knowledge and relevant actions, whereas hate is its shadow and is based on ignorance, separation and alienation. The state of love, acceptance and understanding emanates from the heart or soul and engulfs the self and ego in its wake. God's love is a quality of his original light and creative cosmic energy. Due to love and goodness manifesting in our world, hate and badness appear as shadows and indicators of the original positive attributes. There can be no positive without its equivalent negative.

From different levels of a spectrum of consciousness thought and action are energised by the powers of attraction (love) and repulsion (non-love) or hate.

The instinct for survival in the species implies flexibility, durability and adaptability in changing circumstances. Constant perfection, stability and immortality are the soul's qualities. These are transmitted to the self, which in turn energise the evolving and adapting body and mind. Thus, whoever knows the nature of the self and soul – and their relationship – is indeed most fit to understand the key elements in all of creation. Other knowledges include the unseen subatomic realm, the astrophysical domains and their relationships to our space-time world and the changing realities within its confines and limitations.

The human soul carries the code and patterns of the universe in essence, meaning and appearance. The self's desire for worldly control and dominance is a reflection of the soul's kingdom.

In every desire and action there is a hierarchy of priorities. Personal survival, safety and security are placed before other emotional needs, rational, intellectual or artistic activities such as reflecting upon the beauty of natural surroundings. You need to have good health and clear hearing to appreciate the harmony of a musical performance. Well-being starts with the physical and material ending up with the subtle state of inner consciousness and spiritual health.

All actions are motivated by durable self-interest. Knowledge is sought at numerous levels in order to maintain well-being and contentment.

Every state in creation resonates and vibrates according to a designated range and level of frequency, which reflects and defines its position in nature and its level of consciousness. The bereaved mother will cry at separation from her offspring, the agitated dog will bark, and within the subatomic world particles and energies follow different sets of patterns and destinies. The shell around the seed cracks and withers as the kernel is activated to grow and reproduce its genetic code and fulfil its intended destiny. Every entity in existence has a beginning and an end, grows up and then disintegrates back to its elements within the confines of space-time. The human soul energises the self to evolve through its worldly phase of life and beyond. The self-soul combination carries on after departure from the body towards the hereafter and subtler levels of evolution within a different space-time scale to that of the worldly clock and distance measurement.

Life appears as fragile in its specific worldly manifestations but is durable in its ongoingness. It appears to end, yet it never ends.

Creation on earth is due to the interchange of energy and matter according to numerous designs, patterns, laws, layers and levels. Causes and effects are the strings that hold earthly and heavenly domains connected and unified in dynamic stability. The forbidden tree in the garden of paradise bore the fruits of good and bad, cause and effect. Before adam (adam here denotes the generic name rather than the biblical, hence the lower case) tasted this duality he lived in innocence (or ignorance) without differentiation or discernment. We had to descend to the realm of multiplicity so as to climb the ladders of consciousness back to the ever present unity.

When you experience duality, the light of oneness is out of focus. When you are truly engulfed by unity, you have no notion of duality. The gift to humanity is access to both.

Time appears to flow in a certain direction, yet all natural events and occurrences are simply illusory appearances. As such, they are not stable or absolutely 'true'. The illusion of time and its direction is a common experience due to the confining curvature of our earthly womb of space-time, as well as the mind's association with the senses, memory, the physical body and its biological growth. Personal consciousness, however, is experienced within these confines and awareness of it is due to the pure consciousness of the soul. Personal conditioned consciousness or personality is the offspring of the soul and its constant and pure consciousness.

Truth is independent of all things and events in existence, whereas everything else is dependent upon truth and relates to it. Nothing is possible without truth; not even a lie.

Within the creational web there are numerous levels of connectedness, relationships, attractions and repulsions and the extent of these factors vary within space and time. Every sentient self or entity has a soul that contains its 'software' program. The soul or consciousness of a plant is very limited in scope. Animal consciousness is less complex than human consciousness, which is multifaceted and is potentially connected to cosmic consciousness. For this reason, humankind is the pinnacle of worldly creation; as such, it is most powerful, as well as vulnerable and responsible. The human self can be easily distracted from its natural path of evolution towards its original state of soul beingness and pure consciousness.

Every sentient living entity strives towards the highest level of consciousness that it is capable of. Every entity aspires to its root and origin. Every shadow reveals traces of its light.

The human soul contains all the divine attributes of perfection. These qualities include life, power, will and knowledge. The soul is the energiser and source of life, activating the body, limbs, organs, mind, intellect and all that is considered human. We shall progress to look deeper into the details of the inner and outer maps of human creation, its motivations and drives.

All human endeavours, worldly successes and adventures are futile unless they lead the self to discover the soul and its inner treasures. This is the true spiritual adventure.

The whole universe is brought to life by one divine light, which is reflected, refracted, modified and conditioned by countless interactive movements. Nature functions holistically, in harmony and with ease, but with determination and forcefulness. Earth, water, air and fire are all modes of manifestation with different natural qualities of heat or moisture and other qualities and energies. A flower opens naturally to release its specific fragrance at the most advantageous time for its pollination. A rock rolls off the top of the mountain to rest securely in the valley below. A river flows downward towards the ocean and is recharged by seasonal rain. Human beings desire to experience physical, mental and emotional well-being. Everything in existence seeks stability, whilst the soul is ever-constant, already at peace, always secure and content through its spiritual umbilical cord to god – the ever present light of lights and soul of cosmos.

What is most needed in life is most available and ever present: god's cosmic light, encompassing and permeating existence beyond all limits and within minutiae's.

Life appears as emanation and return, ebbing and flowing. The swings and changes are founded on the eternal truth, which is ever constant and in perfect balance. The beams of luminosity of the one creator and sustainer manifest and radiate as streams of consciousness. Divine consciousness is beyond space-time but permeates existence and gives meaning and direction to all that is in time and beyond. Our access to it is through the soul which is exposed at all times to the golden thread of supreme consciousness.

Stress, strife and desires drive life along and the self towards realisation of the perfect soul. Creation is built upon duality, whilst its foundation is rooted in unity.

Life is a response to the dynamic pulsation of divine sacred presence, which is broadcast by souls and appears as lights and shadows. It is god's perfect qualities which are the threads and beams of energies that hold the cosmos together in dynamic flux. We love power, strength, knowledge, beauty and other names given to god's attributes, which the human intellect can understand and desire. All of these are etched within the soul and call on the self to experience them and be attuned to their presence.

Creation is held by the fields of energies, which relate to attributes within higher consciousness – qualitatively and quantitatively. Human morality or conscience implies access to these.

Life can only be experienced as ever-changing realities. These manifest according to an individual's values, needs, perception and the extent to which personal consciousness is evolved. The web of life is the womb from which every generous gift is born, culminating in the knowledge of the ever-perfect, ever-present essence and source of creation, and sustenance and evolvement in life. The countless twos are suspended by the invisible subtle webs and threads descending and ascending to the one. The cosmic soul is reflected in various levels and degrees in the souls of all creations. It is the light of this essence which bestows the mysterious, yet common, day-to-day human experiences. The ultimate miracle is the amazing possibility that everything is in the one and the one is latent within all.

You may be different and unique as an individual but essentially all human beings have the same aspirations and potential. All human souls are similar but selves differ and change constantly. Harmony between human beings is a function of the self's resonance with its soul.

1.2. UNIFIED OPPOSITES

There is a ceaseless interplay between all opposites in creation. All opposing entities are never apart and each contains the root of the other and need that complementarity.

From ancient times, human beings wondered about cause and effect and the nature of duality and opposites. In ancient Persia, India, China, Greece and elsewhere, the ideas of unity and multiplicity were a part of religion and philosophy. Great thinkers and prophets expounded on duality as the foundation of causality and that all discernable worlds are but outer manifestations of cosmic unity. Paradise, redemption, resurrection and nirvana were often described as liberation from duality. The implication is that peace and tranquillity are qualities of unity and conflict and struggle relate to opposites and dualities.

Everything is revealed through its opposite. Truth is known by falsehood; 'bad' is simply the other side of good. One side is not possible without the other. The truth is one entity but appears with two facets.

Whatever manifests in life is one of two. Every event or manifestation in life moves between two complementary opposites, reinforcing each other and their co-existence. The universe as macrocosm and man as microcosm correspond, relate and reflect each other. Whatever there exists in one is present in the other. We cannot know or discern any entity or quality unless its opposite or mirror image exists: happiness is known by contrast with misery; calmness is opposite to agitation; sweetness offsets bitterness; love of life counterbalances fear of death. Whenever a trait reaches its extremity it reverts to its opposite: good food, for example, when eaten in excess will bring about ill health.

Whatever expands can also contract. Gatheredness is a prelude to separation and divergence can lead to convergence. Meaning appears as a form and vice versa.

At no time can one freeze a state or feeling in the world of perpetual movement and change. You may experience time as slow or fast but the self cannot get out of the space-time dimension, except through the gateway of death or by the occasional glimpse of pure consciousness. We cannot ward off all undesirable events or difficulties, for they are the opposite and counter balance to desirability and inner ease. Once you accept this dynamic situation, you will begin to witness the perfection of the appearance of these diverse realities in existence, irrespective of one's personal state, evaluation or needs.

Strength has its root in weakness, health in illness, light in shadows and darkness. Sound in silence, the tangible in the immaterial.

The wise person will accept the world of interchanging dualities and understand the presence of the constant changeless truth behind them. The soul transmits pure consciousness to the self, which experiences changes and awareness of these opposite experiences through the senses and the mind. Love and hate, beauty and ugliness, contentment and discontentment, friendship and enmity, security and insecurity, knowledge and ignorance, hardship and ease, are all two sides of the same coin, whose invisible metal is pure consciousness or truth. All so-called negative qualities, such as fear, anger, meanness, hatred, or impatience belong to the self and ego, whereas positive qualities, such as courage, generosity or mercy, belong to the soul and can be attained by the mind or self through reference to higher consciousness.

Like all of creation opposites have their roots in the one unique essence and source from which they emanate and to which they return.

All opposing qualities reinforce each other in an exclusive pluralistic partnership. A 'good' is understood as not being 'bad'. Yet what is judged as good today may be seen as bad tomorrow. Every good or bad is relative according to time and place. Virtues or vices can change positions depending upon the context. To be a good listener to others is a virtue which becomes a vice when you lend your ear to a criminal plot or backbiting. Only the essence or truth is ever constant and perfect at all times. It is the foundation which enables all relative entities to appear: like an ocean floor, it is constant, whereas the surface waves rise and subside with varying force.

Countless diversities are sustained in different situations and for different durations by the ever present power of eternal divine unity.

All activities in life are powered by the forces of attraction and repulsion that are felt as love and hate and all human endeavours are directed towards achieving balance and stability in body, mind and soul. As the soul needs the body to manifest, any feeding of the body is tantamount to feeding the soul; thus prayer or acts of worship which relate to the soul help to sustain the body. Thus, eating nourishes the soul while prayers the body – though common belief would have it otherwise. The soul needs the body and the body has no life without its soul.

All human love relates to knowledge and understanding, whereas hate is ignorance and disconnection. Love connects and unifies, hate repulses and despises.

Love, understanding, compassion and harmony are all based upon knowledge and are desirable. Sexual attraction relates to the desire of the self for complementarity and fulfilment by engaging with a human soul-mate so as to lead to the discovery of the permanent inner soul. Discord and enmity relate to ignorance and therefore are repulsive and cause repulsion. From early childhood we are attracted by what is familiar and hate or fear what we do not know. However, most of our values and their priorities change as the self or mind evolves and grows from a childish ego – which only knows instant pleasure and fleeting emotions – to a mature and rational self guided by intellect and wisdom.

Cause and effect are like two mirrors reflecting aspects of each other, sustaining their dual nature. Truth is like the light or energy which connects them.

Since every good and bad are relative and changeable within space-time, we always need to consider the value given to an issue according to the context and situation. The Masai welcoming ceremony for an honoured visitor may appear as threatening to a peasant from India. 'Absolute good' is a unique divine quality (supreme or pure consciousness) that is not subject to worldly wisdom or logic. It has a perfection beyond good or bad – eternally good. At all times human beings seek goodness and security in a world of change whose very nature continually creates new and challenging situations. This paradox is resolved when it is realised that it is only the soul's domain that is ever-secure and the self is always restless.

The term 'evil' implies total badness, whereas in the world of duality everything is relative: there can be no bad without the seed of goodness lying dormant within it.

The soul contains all the patterns of creation and is the source which energises the entire human self. This is why the self loves to explore, discover and know the root causes in life. The self delves into discernable realities and the soul beams truth upon all of these changing realities. Hence it is natural for the self to seek outer power and strength, overlooking the fact that every strength is also accompanied by a weakness. In the outer world, dualities and opposites are inseparable; when they neutralize each other, peace and stability is the outcome. This is depicted by the yin/yang symbol, which contains the design of the two complementary opposites dovetailing into each other, with a speck of the other in its main mass. This graphically symbolises that all dualities contain within themselves the seed of their opposite irrevocably locked in.

Vices and virtues are ever connected to one source, which creates them. Virtues reflect perfections and vices their dark shadows. Turn your back to a vice and you encounter the relevant virtue. A reflective seekers' vice may unlock the door of virtue.

Duality and plurality is at the foundation of human nature and experience. We experience the material, causal, rational and worldly self, as well as the other subtle inner, intangible and non-worldly heart or soul. The exclusive relationship between the constant soul and the restless self is the supreme paradox of life and incentive driving us to knowledge and discovery. For thousands of years, humankind has tried to resolve this inner issue or conflict through reason, meditation, religion and other means. Those who arrived at a satisfactory answer reached it through transformation within consciousness, rather than logic, reason or rational philosophy. This process is called 'self-realisation', or 'enlightenment', and it takes place within the purified heart, where earthly and heavenly domains meet and space-time merges with the timeless. This is also where truth obliterates all identities and boundaries.

Whatever is within your heart will show itself somehow in spite of your desire to conceal it. The outer and inner are always connected and everything in creation emits or expresses an aspect of its state.

If one desires to know the sacred and the unseen worlds then the first steps begin within the physical world of causal patterns and forms. The root of all earthly life is heavenly and the foundation of the material world is spiritual. The light that illumines all is god's unique light from which all other lights, colours and creational patterns emanate. From supreme consciousness pure consciousness and countless spectra of personal consciousnesses emerge.

Creation is based on movement and change emanating from eternal stillness, to which it returns and by which it is sustained. One cosmic soul broadcasting countless earthly ones. One ocean harbouring infinite varieties of life.

The wise seeker knows that no worldly state structure or condition will remain forever. Neither ease nor difficulty have any durability; nor do good and bad, as they always alternate. Focus upon the light that produces the shadows and you will understand the nature and meaning of the images produced without much difficulty. Durable inner joy and bliss is beyond cause or effect, as are all authentic spiritual experiences — flashes of the light of truth or signals from the soul. Outer changes and movements are balanced by the potential of inner stillness and ease. Every effect emanates from a specific cause and all of these unite in the supreme essence.

Expansion is the other side of constriction; wellness is the better side of illness. Knowledge is where there is light and connection and ignorance relates to darkness and uncertainty.

In the human pursuit of knowledge the relevant question triggers the answer, which has always been there but not close at hand. In truth, all causes and effects are connected and united; as are all questions and answers. Although it appears logical to us that the questions precede the answers, the reverse could equally be true. Problems and solutions are not separate: the solution is always part of the problem. Truth, which is where cause and effect, question and answer, are at their origin of unison before separation and discernment. Since we are bound by time and space, our experiences follow chronologically in space. The answer can be found because the question is begging it. 'Eureka' literally means 'I have found it!' A spark of eternal truth has illumined the moment in time. Duality has acknowledged its origin of unity. A flash of tranquillity and peace prevails.

Wherever there is sickness, there too lies the remedy. One can also say that the remedy wanted to be known and therefore sickness appeared. All moments and change seek their resting point. Time exists within timelessness.

Attraction and repulsion relate to acceptance and rejection. When you accept silence, you reject noise. This is also the case with peace/war, pleasure/displeasure, contentment/discontentment, order/chaos, beauty/ugliness, ease/difficulty, agreement/objection, calmness/agitation and other choices and experiences. Greater outer wealth and power is often balanced by lesser inner wisdom and knowledge. More earthly concern implies less heavenly lights. The outer world appears real and secure, although it is in constant flux. The inner world's nature is beyond mental logic and reason for the soul is ever-content and secure. The heart has reason that the mind cannot comprehend.

The more one seeks worldly pleasure, the more elusive will be the discovery of lasting inner joy. One path is based on sensation and the other on inner perception.

The wish for death occurs when the self focuses at the dark side of the inner mirror whose front side shines with the joys of life. The restless self is now confused and has given up the search for the peaceful domain within the heart. Love for living is also often accompanied by distractions, excitements and attachments to earthly life. The awakened ones see this temporary life as a nursery and preparation for the vast world of meanings and spiritual thrills and discoveries. Boundless perfections are present now but are veiled by the illusion of time and conditioned consciousness; 'hell' or 'oblivion' is the state of missing paradise and is experienced as suffering in our own world.

Accepting and submitting to outer limiting boundaries are preludes to insight of the boundless. These two states always occur together and connect within the human heart where intellect and soul meet.

Every experience or event reflects a desirable aspect of a divine quality, such as power, knowledge and life, or the opposite, such as impotence, ignorance and death. When the self is at one with the soul it experiences fulfilment through this union. When it faces the opposite side it experiences the bleakness of the shadowy ego. The unevolved mind or self is closer to its own reflected images and ego than to its soul. The mature self experiences generosity, mercy, patience and other divine qualities as transmitted by the soul when mind and heart are clear. The self (mind or ego) experiences weakness, insecurity, confusion and impatience due to lack of reliable connection to higher intellect and soul consciousness.

Understandable causal connections and reasons lie hidden behind every difficulty and conflict. With insight, order will be discerned within chaos and perfection within what was judged as imperfect.

Life is experienced by movement and change and is perceived

through different levels of consciousness. Death is the zone where outer action and change cease but soul consciousness continues tinted by the cumulative personal consciousness gained through experience and memory. Life has its origin in pre-existence and is the essence and source behind all worldly events, which emanate and return to the same origin. Life before death in this world is ephemeral and confused; after death it is eternal and can be clear and sublime.

In this world we act and know; in the hereafter we cannot act but only know. From the limitations of time and space we step onto the shores of the eternal.

The most basic sets of complementary opposites are inner/outer, meaning/form and earthly/heavenly. Every outer occurrence contains an inner purpose or meaning. Chaos and wars are worldly outer events due to diversity, dispersion and pluralities, whereas peace is heavenly, inner, and reflects gatheredness, connectedness and unity. Every form or shape (a moving fist) betrays a meaning (anger). Everything on earth (terrestrial) has its archetype or pattern in the unseen (heavenly or celestial). Whatever is below represents and reflects that which is above and vice versa. All human attempts and endeavours in this life are to balance these sets of opposites. Maturity and wisdom implies being at the midpoint and at the centre, whilst witnessing the peripherals. The sages, prophets and enlightened beings were the middle-most people, acknowledging outer change whilst focused upon the inner root of absolute stillness.

A fault or vice can be the door to its companion opposite, described as virtue. Otherwise the self will be engulfed in vices and the world becomes hell.

The ancients have described earthly experiences and entities by the four qualities of hot/cold and wet/dry. The earth is cold and dry and is surrounded by water which is cold and wet; then comes air which is hot and moist; then fire which is hot and dry. Stability and harmony occur when these opposite qualities meet and neutralize. Relationships between entities are due to their original unity and connectedness in essence. The yin/yang balance means just that. The earth is the life giver, as well as the life taker. Water is the same; it is the foundation of life, but floods and contaminated water are big takers of life. The brain ceases to function after five minutes without oxygen, but air is also the cause of hurricanes, tornados and other destructive storms. There would be no life on earth without the heat and energy of the sun, yet raging fires destroy much of our forests and drought can turn previously flourishing landscapes into deserts. Heat gives life and destroys it. Earthly life is a fine balance between opposing forces.

The agitation of opposites comes to rest when they meet and reach the state of equilibrium from which they had emerged in the first place.

One traditional world view is that of the heavens being the masculine pole of existence, while the earth under its influence gives birth to all living creatures and thus is the feminine pole. This is another paradigm of parallel dualities. Everything in existence has a qualitative aspect and a quantitative measure. Life's qualitative origin does not lend itself to step-by-step logic and reason, for it belongs to the zone of inner vision not outer division. If we try to reduce the world to quantitative aspects only, our world will be out of balance. We are limited quantitatively and unbounded qualitatively. Human wholesomeness needs to experience both domains.

The universal soul overflows into countless souls and entities. All is within all yet appearing temporarily with distinct identities, personalities and changing shapes and physicalities.

1.3. HEAVEN ON EARTH

The human microcosm with its body, mind, intellect, heart and soul resembles a mobile earthly city or country and a parable of god's kingdom on earth (the macrocosm).

Earthly wisdom is a necessary prelude to heavenly insights and higher wisdom. 'The grass is greener on the other side' may hold some truth on earth. As for paradise, there is only eternally perfect grass. The phrase 'be content with the half full glass' rings hollow for the restless self which is primed to seek the full glass and only constant perfection. The self passionately seeks the overflowing fountain of the soul. No other love can ever make up for this ingrained, primal passion. The self is addicted in its spiritual quest to unite with its soul mate. Deep down everyone is a perfectionist because of the ever-perfect soul but we remain confused and unfulfilled due to lack of unison between self and soul.

The self is drawn to extreme sports or futile attempts to go beyond the limitations of mind and body. The soul is boundless and so the self tries to flee from its earthly cage. The shadow is restless until it surrenders to its source.

Everything in existence is within an energy field pattern or system, interacting with other physical and intangible entities. Every form or shape will disappear in time when its energy and other components return to the original pool. Whatever we strive for in the world is limited in quality, quantity and duration. Yet the self always desires the limitless. Where is the reason and logic in this tendency? The wise seeker will know that all worldly endeavours are elusive and will inevitably lead to some disappointment. Spiritual wisdom is to transcend worldly disappointments and discover heavenly appointments. All our earthly realities and diversities have their root and origin in the heavenly non-tangible state, which dominates the earth and the universe. The unseen is thinly veiled by the seen. This world is only a step towards heavens. The mind is a doorway to the heart. The self is there only to acknowledge the soul. The sublime is veiled by the ridiculous.

There can be no form without a meaning or purpose, no meaning without an appearance in form. There can be no earth without a heaven, no sight without insight, and no truth without a lie.

Symmetry underlies the worldly laws within time and space. Throughout the world, the human preoccupation with discovering these laws has given rise to useful paradigms and analogies, with considerable overlap and similarities. The Chinese culture placed the root of all duality and multiplicities in the creative force of Tao — the dark yin containing a speck of yang and vice versa, each containing the embryonic germ of the other. All these opposing principles are never apart but in continuous interplay as part of the whole. In the Buddhist tradition *nirvana* is liberation from the opposites, where the world of duality vanishes into unity. The central theme in most Middle Eastern religions is the concept of all emanating from One and returning to it.

Truth or absolute reality is god. The soul is a reflector of that primary reality and the self is a secondary, dependent and changing reality.

Life pulsates between the two poles of meaning and form, action and intention, consciousness and unconsciousness. Death is the point at which this motion ceases and a new dimension of 'singular' or unified state begins. The afterlife is where knowledge and consciousness are not connected to action, where self and soul are not separate and where the material entities are not veiling their true meanings and realities. There is a new clarity and knowledge with no confusion or distraction.

When the self becomes aware of the fantasy of its independence, the person is at the threshold of accepting the eternal soul and uniting with it.

Every event or experience fits within the spectrum of the earthly/heavenly grid. The self is earthly: experiences begin and end and relate to whatever is material, causal, discernable and definable. The soul is non-material, eternal, heavenly, unseen, intangible, subtle, and follows patterns of logic and reason which are totally different to earthly logic and rationality. Everything that is discernable or definable has a beginning and an end; yet whatever is on earth has its original pattern, design or blueprint in the unseen or intangible domain. These two domains co-exist and complement each other as two parallel universes. There is nothing in creation without its parallel equivalent. In natural science and physics, parallel universes are a noticeable feature implying simple or complex systems mirroring or echoing each other. This phenomenon is part of the nature of duality, multiplicity and symmetry in creation.

The earth is like a virtual reality of the heavens. The self is also a virtual reality of the soul. Truth is like the permanent screen upon which all these projections take place.

The following list compares earthly experiences with heavenly ones: changing/constant; limited/unlimited; tangible/intangible; structured/amorphous; separate and dispersed/united and gathered; outer/inner; form/meaning; uncertain/certain; temporary/permanent; dependent/independent; stressful/ easy; conditioned-consciousness/ pure-consciousness; physical/ metaphysical; limited/transcendent; seen/unseen; insecure/

secure. The list is endless.

Beautiful objects are forms reflecting the inner meaning or primal pattern of beauty itself – a divine quality known to the soul and desired by the self. The seeker loves permanent beauty, not a perishable beautiful object.

The sculpture of a hero's head is a form whose meaning is to remember the special qualities of the person concerned. Swelling in the foot is an 'outer', earthly form whose message is the need for 'inner' care in order to reduce 'earthly' pain and thereby bring about 'heavenly' ease. Every event or experience in life can be described by these dynamic complementary opposites, which are connected in outer experience as well as in essence. The human soul was designed in the heavens and the earthly experiences of the self complete the unification of this creational duality and restore everything back to unity.

Earthly evolution is to do with 'becoming', whereas 'beingness' is heavenly and thus has no beginning or end: it simply is. The earth is the doorway to the heavens as is the mind to the heart.

All human beings love the divine qualities of beauty, majesty, power, generosity, unconditional love, ever-lastingness, self-sustenance and all other perfect attributes. We desire clear eyesight, good hearing, a sharp mind and an agile body to appreciate these excellent traits. For deeper insights we need a purified wholesome heart. All these desirable qualities make the 'earthly' self seek its 'heavenly' soul partner.

The soul is the source of all divine qualities and attributes including sight, beauty, ability and other knowledges relating to earth and heavens.

Our love for exploring truth includes the desire to discover the root and purpose of self awareness and ego. When images and mental values do not flow or evolve they give the impression of mental durability and sustenance to the self, enhancing the illusion of independence and the reality of 'self image' or personality. At first the seeker is veiled; later on one recognises the purpose of the veil and leaves it behind. An outer boundary or identity is there to lead one back to the original pool of sacred entity.

Our love for keeping secrets relates to safeguarding the mysterious soul within. Our love for discovering secrets is the desire of the self to know the soul.

Love for earthly wealth is a natural human desire whose meaning is to attain ease in material life, power, security and influence. Action is an earthly form whose purpose is to unlock meaning and knowledge. Acting with the appropriate intention and discipline will lead to wider or higher knowledge, which in turn can bring about better and more effective future actions. Every creation, atom, mineral, plant and animal are subject to the dynamic interchange between energy and matter expressed in meaning and form, inner and outer, earth (tangible) and heaven (unseen).

Worldly achievement is like climbing a mountain: the higher you are the more vulnerable you become. Inner wisdom and growth is the reverse: the deeper you dive, the safer it is.

Every entity – simple or complex, mineral, vegetative or living – has within it an evolving 'software' programme that activates it from birth to death. The cat which has just given birth fights intruders to protect its kittens but will lash out at its adult offspring later on when the grown up kittens compete for the mother's food. The cat simply acts appropriately in different situations unaware of the workings of its mind and its complex system of chemicals, hormones and electromagnetic currents. Life's experiences are the result of tangible 'earthly' and subtle 'heavenly' interaction. This occurs at multiple levels, within the individual being as well as within the environment at large. All of these forces act naturally and in perfect harmony and ease. Consciousness and awareness manifest differently according to the changing contextual interplay of self and soul and the outer environment.

The constant and eternal truth is like a permanent screen or mirror which allows worldly occurrences to flash upon it, only to disappear again and be replaced by new images.

The human brain stores images, values, emotions and their meanings at different memory levels, networks and circuits, with different degrees of durability and accessibility. What we pull out of these files is in accordance with the experiences at hand, the personal physical and psychological state and the evolvement of consciousness. If, from past experiences, one remembers a mother's preference for one's younger sibling, it is likely that one will selectively notice her giving special attention to that sibling, reinforcing the old emotional experience of jealousy. The emotional self (mind) tends to confirm the inner mental images or values already selected, whether positive or negative. The self and mind always seek security and continuity, which are the innate qualities the soul possesses. In truth each of us desire what the soul has. To know this and put it into practice is the object of spiritual education. The result is personal transformation.

Mind without rationality is a crude un-evolved state, and heart without wisdom and intellect is simply innate potential. Mind and heart complete the unison of soul and self.

The mind has a built-in bias to reinforce the familiar and perpetuate self identity. The same biased principle applies to societies with their cultural habits, norms and expectations. Through repetitive events or reminders we bring about the illusion of social stability and security to the individual self, as well as to society. This phenomenon is also at the root of the feeling that time flows in one direction as though it were a river.

The most persistent veils of truth are what the self considers to be important or true which are often simply reinforcement of past likes, dislikes and ego.

The human soul is an 'inner', 'unseen' and 'heavenly' entity whose meaning and purpose is to energise and develop its companion self (and mind) to perfect alignment with it and thus bring completion and wholesomeness to the human being. The soul is self-sustaining, eternally stable and heavenly. It embraces and nourishes the earthly self so that the person desires and experiences harmony and perfections in the world, irrespective of outer events and situations. The soul carries the imprint of perfect paradise and the self yearns for this blissful state.

The self is like the moon whose light and movement is due to its sun, the soul. This duality brings about the desired unity once this truth is recognised and accepted.

The desire of the self to take on the quality of the soul drives it towards higher consciousness and spiritual wisdom. Human prejudices or changing perspectives are due to the self's desire to experience perfection in every instance and everywhere, which is the state of the soul. We constantly seek heavenly experiences whilst still bound to earth. The restless self can attain peace and contentment only when it submits to the soul in the abode of the purified heart. It is here where personal conditioned consciousness unifies with pure soul consciousness that heaven and earth unite in harmony.

All outer intentions and actions are fundamentally motivated and driven by the self's desire to achieve inner harmony and contentment. Only then has one a share of happiness.

1.4. LIGHTS OF CONSCIOUSNESS

Every awareness or consciousness is a flash of light energised by the supreme universal light. In the animal kingdom, the soul emits this energy and brings about life. There are countless levels and spectrums of consciousnesses within the universe.

Consciousness is the primary power, which brings about sentiency to created beings which, enables them to become aware and to be able to respond to stimuli. Pure consciousness is like invisible light before refraction and reflection into colours and shades. It is the primal power and source of consciousness, awareness and experience. The human soul receives and emits this special form of energy which in turn is modified, conditioned and produces personal consciousness It is personal or conditioned consciousness which gives individuality and specific qualities and identity to a creation. The soul is the connecting point between personal-conditioned consciousness and the eternal-supreme-divine consciousness, Godhead or cosmic soul.

Soul consciousness is like a spark from god's cosmic light: it produces personal consciousness, which evolves to the ultimate realisation of the one source behind and within all realities and creations.

Like electric power, pure consciousness energises specific or personal consciousness such as a light bulb or a specific heater. When pure consciousness becomes modified, refracted, reflected or transformed it manifests as conditioned or defined consciousness. Light has two manifestations: photons and electro-magnetic waves. So do human beings: a self with a specific identity and life (like a photon) and a soul, which is an energy wave with no definable life span and is non spatial. The electro-magnetic wave is the energy field in which the photon appears and disappears; the self and its identity grow and depart within the field of soul consciousness. As the self grows to spiritual maturity it comes to the realisation of soul essence or higher (pure) consciousness, as well as its transient and conditioned identity and physical characteristics. When self and soul are in unison, the ultimate human purpose is achieved.

Pure consciousness, the soul and the inner heart are not subject to space-time limitations, whereas the self and mind are. Their meeting point is in the wholesome heart.

Human evolution and growth of wisdom or spiritual intelligence can be described by the extent and quality of self awareness, responsibility and higher consciousness. The broader and deeper is a person's knowledge and wisdom, the greater is the potential realisation of the unifying power of the divine supreme light, which is the thread of stability and harmony in creation. By this light and knowledge, the individual person realises the universality of the self and soul, their inseparability and dependence upon each other and the path of salvation. Physical growth and mental development are preludes to the person's evolvement from conditioned consciousness to the pure consciousness of the soul. This spiritual growth and wakefulness is a major factor in one's behaviour and quality of life. When the pure heart leads then a healthy mind is likely to follow and the result is most likely to be appropriate behaviour and conduct.

An optimum state of harmony is attained when consciousness of self (body, mind, intellect) is in alignment with soul consciousness.

Human thought is like a flowing river with a sentient riverbed. Sometimes the water seems to move slowly and at other times swiftly; it may be turbulent, calm, clear, murky, meandering, or cascading. States of wakefulness and dreams are like different rivers, where past, present and future waters (emotions and thoughts) blend, connect and flow again in different directions. The river bed (personal consciousness) evolves and registers the waters that flow above it. Intellect and the higher rational mind connect and link diverse entities whilst seeking the root of unity and pure consciousness.

The evolved self reflects upon and can benefit from dreams and their meanings, whereas the ordinary person often regards dreams as disturbed sleep and confusion.

All human understanding, knowledge or experience occur in reference to previous images, ideas or values stored in the mind. We perform a constant matching and alignment between what is freshly experienced with relevant past memory and values, consciously or unconsciously. The brain's neural networks begin to develop with early childhood experiences and these are modified with old age. No experience occurs without double-takes or mirroring. Even at the level of brain function, there are two aspects to memory: one is the actual storage and processing of an event, the other is its retrieval.

Memory also occurs due to both sight (pictorial memory) and verbal (sound memory). There is a constant process of auditing , change and updating of a person's memory images, value and emotional references, outlook on life and personal objectives.

A thought comes to mind in relationship to a similar or contrasting stimulus, like a spark that sets alight a ready candle.

It is ironic that a highly conditioned mind is often considered to be healthy and strong. To have a flexible or hesitant mind is considered a personality weakness and thus undesirable. However, a well adjusted and healthy person is 'open-minded' and may consider any point of view as temporary, changeable and subject to review. Mental flexibility can enable one to evolve to higher consciousness. The human mind, memory and senses have evolved to enable us to deal efficiently with the outside world with sufficient flexibility and least 'strong-headedness'. Higher consciousness is the function of the heart, which is endowed with intuition and insights beyond the 'rational' mind. The language of the heart belongs to the soul and pure consciousness.

When you view existence and creation through soul consciousness, you will witness perfect realism beyond mysticism and fatalism.

Childhood memories of images, feelings and perceptions remain deeply engrained within the mind and usually resurface strongly with old age. The pleasant childhood memory of a sweet cookie with a particular flavour triggers off the desire to reproduce those early pleasures and the emotions associated with them. Early memories of unusual, rare or significant events, be they happy or sad, tend to be entrenched in the mind as retrievable long-term memories. By extension, our world-view is very much a function of both personal and cultural exposures to past habits, traditions and value systems. Consequently, the make up of a personality is coloured and conditioned by societal memories and norms. The collective mind's power and influence upon individuals is generally underestimated. Social resistance to change is much stronger than personal intransigence.

A healthy mind is willing to reinterpret and evaluate the outer world and change its 'mindset'. By changing attitude and language, perception changes and the self becomes more flexible and subtle.

We wish to remember, as well as to forget, aspects of our past. The soul knows the truth and is beyond remembrance and forget-fulness. The self deeply desires constancy and boundlessness and

33

thus sometimes seeks oblivion and freedom from limitations and responsibility perversely. Without mental memory the self has no reference to which to relate and assess the new experiences, in order to understand and evaluate them and then decide on an appropriate action. A rational mind is able to deal with an issue sensibly by relating and comparing with relevant situations. Thus, it can read new facts and events more beneficially and reliably. The rational mind's assessment of a situation is as good as the extent of its reference to higher consciousness. Emotional maturity and spiritual growth implies greater reliance on the rational mind, intellect, the heart and higher consciousness.

If you look with the eye of pure consciousness at any event or situation, you will see the full picture and only witness perfection; it could not be different — therefore a perfect fit.

To erase a specific memory we need to reduce the importance and the value ascribed to it and replace that particular recall with a higher meaning or the lesson learned from it. My memory and fear of repeating a painful self-induced accident will make me more careful and aware, hopefully without being nervous or despondent. A healthy person often sheds past mental habits and moves past undesirable tendencies, especially those charged with emotion, grudges and expectations. For the self to evolve to higher consciousness it needs to embrace rationality, and then to listen and follow the heart and soul.

The more one is self concerned and occupied with a specific role, identity, personal image or position, the less one is able to listen to the heart or soul and act appropriately.

Personal consciousness enables us to sense, relate, understand and experience changes and events, within and outside of us. This consciousness is the power behind awareness of physical entities, as well as our own mental processes and ability to discern the inner and outer, feelings and thoughts. A rigid or 'closed' mind retards the evolvement of the self towards its fulfilment. Our habitual thoughts, as well as subconscious tendencies (such as imaginary fears, delusions and concerns) exercise a major influence over our attitude in life and behaviour. Pleasure arises due to experiencing what the self considers desirable and good. Displeasure is simply experiencing what is considered to be disagreeable. Both values can and will change their positions under different circumstances.

The heart is the door to the highest levels of consciousness (as it is the abode of the soul) and it gives rise to personal conditioned consciousness relating to body, mind and senses.

Reading and interpreting events, facts or situations are subjective and differ from one person to another, as well as change with time. It is natural to compare what we see, hear or sense with what is already in our memory of the past. We often try to reinforce what we already know – due to the self's tendency towards perpetuating familiarity of the past – rather than accepting the challenge of new information. The incessant desire for certainty often results in rigidity, closed mindedness and hardness at heart. Déjà vu occurs when conditioned consciousness transmits the sensation of a new experience (in split milliseconds) as though it is from the memory.

Fear of the unknown is often more disturbing than fear of what is a fact. What is already known is limited, but what is unknown seems boundless.

Most thoughts, emotions and experiences occur due to a comparison between two events, values or situations. The exercise of discrimination, logic and rationality will increase mental agility and wisdom. There is, however, another level of discernment or awareness that takes place when the light of insight and soul consciousness shines upon different views, values and entities. The first intelligence is based on reason and intellect; the second emanates from the heart and soul and can be labelled as spiritual intelligence. The first level relates to the changing waves on the ocean and the second relates to the state of the entire ocean and its wholeness.

Mind is the connector to the outer world while heart connects self and soul with the eternal divine essence.

Personal consciousness has qualitative and quantitative aspects. The more one is aware of specific detail, the less one captures the overall picture. The reverse is also true: when you capture the whole picture as in day-to-day activities, one misses out on exact details. The memory is often hazy with regard to details unless either visually or verbally a specific aspect is enhanced or reproduced.

Short-term memory is fragile and can fade away unless it has a special or important impact or is recalled and reinforced by repetition.

The universality of the illusion that time flows is due to personal consciousness identifying with body and mind, which are subject to growth and evolvement in time. The common feeling that time flows in one direction is due to the firing of neurons, which enables 'snapshots' of events to be strung together like a movie. The beginning of cosmos and the 'big bang' of creation is echoed in the human conception in the womb. The start of personal chronological time begins with birth and ends with death. What we experience in life are flashes of movement which occur as a result of the interaction between a thought or event and their impact upon the brain and their relationship with a previous imprint. When a specific awareness is referred to the higher consciousness, the resultant comparison is a more reliable and appropriate interpretation of the particular situation. This process is spiritual wisdom or ultimate rationality.

Higher consciousness reveals aspects of truth veiled behind numerous realities which impact upon the conditioned personal consciousness.

Higher consciousness is beyond the specific physical form or mental awareness and sense. It is the realm of pure meanings and subtle connected patterns. Conditioned consciousness is the first step where all cognition and perceptions occur after modification. With evolvement these insights are flashed across to the intellect with aspects of truth and primal patterns beyond space and time. It is the light of the soul which enables the self to discover perfection in all the dynamics of inner/outer, meaning/form and other dualities. Truth and its ever perfect presence bestows its light upon temporal events when personal and pure consciousness are in unison.

States of higher consciousness are like beams of light, revealing subtle aspects of realities and patterns in existence beyond the 'hard' and material — like an x-ray penetrating through objects.

Dreams occur when different streams of the conscious mind, the subconscious mind and memory meet to be reconciled and relate. Dreams are in a sense more real than the waking world, for they do not pretend to be solid or durable, whereas the so-called 'real world' appears permanent or reliable whilst it is actually in a state of flux and change between forms and energies. Dreams can reveal much about the state of the self and its evolvement, as it mirrors aspects of the person's mental and inner state. A dream may contain a deep message that can help to redress inner distractions or give indications of future directions. It is critical to have insightful and relevant interpretations. A dream needs to be decoded correctly.

Although consciousness is not a material entity it is nevertheless invoked by the physical world, as well as being bound up with language, sensation and perception.

Like other mysteries in our life, the full nature of consciousness is not clearly definable or known. The word itself has been used in numerous contexts and can thus cause much confusion. There are countless levels of personal consciousness involving the outer and inner, body and mind, the basic senses, emotional and rational intelligence. Self consciousness and ego arises when images and ideas are trapped in a brain circuit and become a fixed or regular mental feature. Generally the breadth and depth of a person's awareness and consciousness relates to 'presence of mind' or general intelligence. Spiritual intelligence refers more to pure consciousness beyond the specific and discernable.

The highest consciousness relates to the inner heart and the soul within it. It is boundless and immortal and akin to flashes of genius or revealed knowledge.

Spiritual evolvement depends on the extent of reference to higher consciousness, rather than be restricted to mind and memory and basic rationality. The spectrum of personal consciousness is rooted in pure consciousness as transmitted by the soul, to energise the self and its appendages of body, mind, senses and ego. The object of every seeker is to bring into synchrony personal consciousness with soul consciousness. When this state is attained, then optimum harmony between outer situations and personal responses is achieved. Mental agitations come to rest upon the soul's bedrock of truth. The relative and transient become acceptable as they draw authority from the absolute.

To expand your consciousness exercise thoughtlessness and sensory inertness. Just be. The self is only the outer reflector of the soul within.

Every thought has a limited span of reality and implies a separation between the thinker and the thought. This fundamental duality is the foundation of experiential cause and effect. Whereas all thoughts are limited and bring about personal limitations, the potential of one's consciousness is vast for it connects with pure consciousness of the soul, which is itself beyond all limitations. Thoughts are memory based and thus relate both to the past and its relationship to the present and projections to the future. The ego relates to trapped thoughts within the mind like a black hole that sucks in whatever comes to it. The ego asserts itself without regard for anything else.

The mind links the outer world to the memory, emotions and intellect. The heart links the intellect and conditioned consciousness to the soul. The self is the outcome of the state of all of these relationships.

Personal consciousness gives rise to mental or intellectual discrimination, rational evaluation and the so-called objective view. Soul consciousness produces a capacity to witness that is beyond a person's normal mental or emotional sphere. There are two types of witnessing: the personal judging, which is concerned with preservation and continuity, and the clear impersonal witnessing of the moment and all the forces at play in that instant. The first type is politics and the second type is based on gnosis through the heart and is rare.

Awareness of awareness is endless as it connects to higher consciousness. Specific awareness, however, is spatial and short lived.

The self loves the light and power of pure consciousness and is addicted to it. Pure light, however, cannot be discerned or described, save through its manifestation as colours and shades; similarly pure consciousness is transmitted by the soul and manifests as conditioned personal awareness and life. Although this pure light is always present it can only be experienced through conditioned personal consciousness, according to the state of self, mind and body and their alignment to the heart.

Every consciousness or awareness depends (to a degree) upon pure consciousness and relates to it. Every transient reality depends upon the constant truth. Every shadow depends upon light.

2. ADAMIC COSMOLOGY

The soul is a sacred entity within the human heart and is exposed to the world of space-time and beyond, hence it has the imprints of both heaven and earth.

The power of the soul's consciousness activates personal consciousness and self awareness, its wide range and levels creating the tree of life. Soul consciousness relates to supreme consciousness, which is the eternal and absolute truth. This truth is the driving force leading you beyond basic causal knowledge, which is mostly situated in relationships and dualities. Real creativity is close to truth and is based on intuition, not accumulated information. Truth contains vast potential knowledge, infinite creativity and possibilities. It is boundless.

Human experiences are due to the presence of personal consciousness, which causes the self and body to evolve and mature along with emotions, reasoning and rationality. The ultimate purpose of life is to bring about the appropriate unison between the self and the soul. As the composition of the human being is both earthly and heavenly (physical and metaphysical), the self will experience all worldly possibilities, whereas the soul is like a perfect hologram representing and reflecting the divine light and truth. Like a spark containing the characteristics of fire, so is the soul to god. The self, on the other hand, is the soul's accompanying image or shadow which can lead to the abyss of ego or to the vistas of the soul. Nature intends the self to evolve beyond identification with the body, mind and senses, and get close to the heart where the soul resides. The paradox of living with limitations and duality is resolved when access to the soul's boundless perfection takes place. When peace prevails in one's personal kingdom it can also appear in other earthly domains.

The human make-up encompasses the physical/ material/

causal, as well as the subtle/indiscernible spiritual realms. We are thus universal beings challenged by the confinement of 'worldly', 'practical' or 'natural' reductionism. We need to reconnect the self with the soul through the heart to attain optimum quality of authentic personality and joyful living. Man and god are never separate and cannot function independently. We are heavenly creatures evolving on earth so as to realise our true origin and meaning. The journey of the self begins with ignorance and confusion, but can potentially end with union in divine fusion. All is perfect as it has always been and this world of challenges and difficulties is designed for us to accept and surrender to the ever perfect present moment.

The innate nature of the human being is spiritual and heavenly. The body, mind and senses are temporary appendages and faculties adapted for the worldly journey.

2.1. PRIMAL BLUEPRINT

All human souls are similar in essence but each self differs, changes and evolves. Life's purpose and drive is for the self to recognise its essence and goal that lie within the soul, then to surrender to it and witness its perfections.

Soul consciousness emanates like a spark from supreme consciousness. Personal consciousness, or the individual's life force, emanates from the soul and evolves as a hologram in the making. This personal conditioned consciousness energises and activates the multitudes of systems in the body, mind and other human faculties. The mental process begins with the basic recognition of movement, change, sensations, feelings and perceptions. Further development is towards higher intelligence and rationality, connecting mind with heart and the light of the pure consciousness therein.

Whatever 'makes sense' or 'does not' relates to the mind and conditioned consciousness. Transformative knowledge and truth is beyond senses and intellect and relates to soul consciousness.

The self's conditioned consciousness grows and evolves through numerous levels of sensing, feeling, understanding of meanings, wisdom and insights. Relating and interacting with other creation is necessary for developing the senses, mind, ego, memory and access to heart. As personal consciousness grows and deepens, it seeks the higher level of pure consciousness where perfection lies. Beyond logic, reason and intellect lies intuition, insight and inspiration. The limitation of space-time yield to a zone that is on the edge of eternity.

The childish self is commanded by the ego while the evolved self follows the lights emanating from the soul through the inner heart.

Every entity in existence draws its identity and life force from the one divine universal soul, which contains and sustains all individual souls. Each creation grows from the same air and water to unfold the specific innate patterns encoded within it. The same boundless ocean contains every colour, shape, size of separate species and entities, living and dying in groups and clusters within interactive fields of energy and matter. Every creation reveals its individual character and identity by the language and messages it transmits to establish its position within the ever changing natural quilt work of emanation and return.

The soul constantly transmits unconditioned love and calls to the self to unite with it at both mind and heart.

What sets the human self apart from other creations is its capacity to understand and empathise with the ways in which other creations live, develop and die. The self has a unique ability to interact appropriately in the world to its advantage and yet has the capacity to access higher consciousness. Due to these abilities, human beings have a greater responsibility and accountability on earth. The capacity of higher consciousness brings with it the constant need to ensure balance and fairness in all actions and undertakings. This is some form of stewardship that comes as inseparable from the freedom to act and is the foundation of ethical behaviour and outer boundaries.

The soul of Adam is higher than that of other creations, including angels.

It is said that: 'god created man in his own image'. If god is the light of lights then he has no shape or image as such. He can only be known through his attributes and great qualities, which human beings desire to have. It is nevertheless considered godly when the self acts generously, compassionately and patiently. These are divine colours or 'images' which can be draped over personal conduct to varying degrees. It is also ungodly when the self acts meanly, impatiently, ignorantly and hatefully. These negative traits are egoistic and belong to lower self states. The ego reinforces the lower self whilst it disturbs and confuses the rational self, whereas the soul gives hope, positive energy and transmits god's qualities.

The human soul is god's reflection upon the self which is the soul's earthly companion and shadow. Self realisation is the process of self surrender to the soul.

Man's imaginal faculty enables consciousness to perceive solid forms like a table or chair. These solids are in fact energies, which have temporarily taken on forms during space-time transitions. The desirable attributes and qualities which are embedded in our soul are numerous and include love, mercy, generosity, power, hearing, seeing, beauty and majesty. These divine qualities are like beams of light energy manifesting in the world of space-time with different characteristics. The soul contains these imprints like a hologram reproducing its original source. In turn, the self takes these patterns from the soul and experiences aspects of them at different times.

All worldly experiences are outer layers of inner meanings. The allegory of adam and eve descending from heavens down to earth implies that their consciousness contains all that there is in heavens and earth.

The human self always desires lasting goodness and ease and aspires towards excellence. The atom's goal is stability; the plant's is to survive, grow, bear fruit and propagate. In addition to the mineral and vegetative states, animals desire to reach the highest possibility in evolvement as inscribed within their soul. The human self is also on a journey of discovery of the timeless and boundless soul, but through the smooth and rough worldly terrain of pluralities and space-time limitations.

The self's need for identity, belonging and being known or loved is a universal drive in mankind. The soul is ever-known, acknowledged and loved by its essence (or God or its creator); the self desires this reality and certainty.

With spiritual growth the self begins to realise that perfection pervades every situation and experience in existence, even disturbed or chaotic events. It is natural for the self to connect cause and effect and aspire toward the original source of all causes. When the self witnesses the direct, instantaneous and constant connection between all causes and all effects, it has intuitively reached the unifying ocean of truth. This is the intense moment when time and space freeze in awe of eternity and boundlessness.

When the self leaves aside the ego and self-image it begins to receive illuminations and higher insights from the heart.

The self's ability to discern dualities is due to its conditioned consciousness whose origin is the soul consciousness. The young self also swings between shadows of the ego and lights of the soul, vices and virtues, agitation and contentment. The evolving self is in constant pursuit of witnessing the outer perfection (as in the world) as well as inner bliss (as in the soul). Mistakes or vices are the dark side of the self but, if understood, can lead to the doors of virtues which open into the illumined courtyard of the heart.

The childish self naturally rebels to assert its elusive freedom. The groomed self simply submits to its authentic companion – the soul. It is thereby set free from the desire of unattainable worldly freedom. Spiritual wisdom is the realisation of no choice except that which is optimum at that moment.

The natural drives of attraction and repulsion energise a hierarchy of needs, starting with physical preservation and safety, followed by emotional satisfaction, then social and other needs. These lead towards self-fulfilment and contentment in the soul's abode. The love of exploration beyond boundaries, defying dangers and taking risks are part of the self's restless search for the boundless soul. We crave for instant 'outer' satisfaction, which is instigated by the ever present 'inner' satisfied soul within the heart. All tendencies and natural drives of the self are intrinsically motivated by the search for the soul-mate within.

When the self is consumed with its passion for truth and has lost its identity, it is at the door of the beloved, who gives it comfort and the balsam of unity. There is always ONE.

All human desires and needs follow the patterns and qualities embedded within the soul. The self can only reach contentment by yielding and submitting to the soul and being in unison with it. Only then can it witness perfection of the present moment and every other moment. Heavenly perfection is cast upon the earth for those who can resonate with it along the spiritual journey. Anything other than this unison is distracting and disappointing. The determined seeker keep only one appointment: timeless bliss.

The self's desire for power, knowledge, wealth, immortality and other attributes are simply flashes of the treasury within the soul being glimpsed through the heart.

The outer world and a person's inner state mirror each other. When there is synergy and alignment, harmony and peace are experienced. Outer disturbance will make the self attempt to change the world, leave it or drive the wise self to seek its source and find the root of contentment within. The powers of attraction or repulsion enable the self to steer towards the abode of peace and tranquillity in the outer world as well as within the illumined heart.

When you say this matter touches your heart you mean that it is deep, powerful and beyond the mind. It relates to the sacred soul.

It is divine justice and generosity that all human souls are similar in essence, whereas every self and ego differs and changes. In what matters most human beings have the same potential and in what is worldly and is changing we are all different. The human heart links the heavenly unseen soul with its earthly evolving self. The youthful self is like a wild and restless horse, which needs to be broken in and trained so that it grows in experience and wisdom to listen to its heart and soul. The delivery of self to soul starts with a disciplined mind and intellect and ends with union at heart.

The desires of the self never end, for how can you match limited earthly gains and pleasures with the heavenly abundance within the soul's abode?

Shame, regret and guilt occur when the self acts in a way that is too distant from the equivalent qualities within the soul. The soul is ever perfect and the self's mistakes or vices show its short-coming and drives it through intellect and reason to improve through self awareness and accountability. Absentmindedness implies lack of presence or reference to high consciousness. Being 'caught in a hurry' or 'out of sorts' implies a lack of inner referencing. The self always wants to take more than it gives, whereas the soul only overflows with divine generosity. The needs of the self cannot be satisfied while the soul is ever-content.

Discontentment with the lower self or ego is part of natural growth, which could lead to contentment with the higher self or soul. Less ephemeral is more eternal.

It is a great illusion that the faster one moves in life the richer or fuller our life becomes. This is due to the fantasy desire to go beyond the limitation of space-time. The self is ever impatient because the soul's nature is timeless and boundless, although it is temporarily acting within space-time to provide life to the evolving self. Infinite speed implies a futile attempt to transcend the natural worldly limitations to the zone of the soul, where everything is potentially possible instantaneously as there are no bounds or restrictions. When a child is born, it still naturally resonates with the soul, as it does not experience or understand the concept of time yet. For an old person, used to worldly limits, being patient for several months is naturally understandable. For a three-year-old child, a year is a third of its life; for a sixty-year-old, it is not that long. For the self (or mind) all measures are relative, yet it seeks the absolute.

Chronological mental traps are the ego's nests and nurseries producing self image and identity.

Whenever a specific desire is achieved, the self experiences contentment and momentary peace – reflecting the permanent state of tranquillity and the contentment of the soul. The self operates in a closed loop of desiring, achieving and then acting again to fulfil new desires. This process never ends and echoes the eternal blissful state of the soul to which the self aspires but never achieves in its outer pursuits. It is only through abandonment of the illusion of the self's independence or separation from the soul that union and ease begins. Life's real project is to make outer personal projects preludes to the real and worthwhile inner project.

The nature of the self is to be in need and to fulfil desires. The root of this state is for the self to discover its original and primal need to submit and unite with its soul contentedly.

The soul within every sentient entity acts as a compass steering the being towards its altar, which is where its purpose in life lies. An ant's expression of worship is through dedicated service to communal survival and growth. A cat's altar is comfort, ease and playful carefree living. A domesticated dog needs a human psyche with which to align its consciousness; its focus is the owner's command or wish – then its dog consciousness is attuned to its highest potential. Life on earth is based on the constant movement of entities to attain their highest state and thereby achieve stability. Our world is god's laboratory and resembles the ancient alchemical workshop where base metals are transmuted to gold.

Every soul is most beautiful and perfect but veiled behind the self and personality. Take the self away and you face the ultimate perfection in creation.

2.2. THE HUMAN PARADOX

The human soul is the highest in creation; its shadow companion, the self, wishes to be in that position. At best it can be as the moon is to the sun, simply reflecting some of its light.

Who am 'I'? The greatest puzzle and mystery in human life is that each person refers to the self as 'I', which implies a defined and constant entity; yet every self changes continually – physically, mentally, emotionally. How can a person be constantly the same, yet changing? What are the dynamics of this enigmatic shifting constant?

When the self reaches its most restless confusion it may be at the door of the soul's peaceful abode.

This great paradox will dissolve by the discovery that human nature comprises two divergent entities belonging to different cosmological domains. One entity is the self, which is earthly, with physical and outwardly definable aspects. The other is the soul, which is the seat of consciousness and the source of life; it is 'heavenly', unseen and intangible. The earthly self is identified by body, mind, senses and intellect; it has specific unique characteristics and personality. The physical dimension contains all the organs, glands, and the mind with all other subtle connection programmes, memory, emotions and intellect.

The shadow of the sacred soul is the profane self. This duality is at the core of every human being.

The inner senses contain the recall systems – memories with stored values and desires which help to preserve and develop the self past the physical domain towards the heart and the effulgent soul. Thoughts are discernable in relation to the background of stillness or no-thought. All mental activities are movements which begin and end and relate to outer events or situations via the senses of the self. This is how awareness or specific consciousness takes place.

All thoughts arise due to conditioned consciousness and are rationalised by referencing memory and higher consciousness. Thoughts are energy streams in separation seeking gatheredness.

The connecting point of our two distinct domains is the heart, where the rational self meets higher consciousness. Using the colour paradigm, the blue end of the self's spectrum meets the red end of the soul's. The uniqueness of the human being is its spectrum of consciousness which covers the gross specific aspects of the material world and consciousness relating to subtle intangible realities. The sublime and the ridiculous meet in the breast of the human being. We can be less than an ape and higher than an angel. We are both earthly and heavenly. This is the ultimate paradox and constant challenge to individuals and society. The question can never be resolved, just dissolved when the restless self meets its restful soulmate.

The relationship of the human soul to god is like a drop of the ocean carrying the oceanic secrets, or like a spark from the cosmic light with all its universal possibilities.

The childish self is preoccupied with outer care and its awareness is focused upon the physical body, senses and material things. Taste, touch, smell, sight and sound are the main channels of contact with the world outside. Emotional development is based on relating memories and experiences of the past to new experiences and synthesising a new outcome. With discipline and grooming the mind experiences rationality, higher creativity and occasional intuition and insight. Slowly with spiritual wisdom there will be more guidance from the heart, rather than the head.

The self always desires happiness / wealth / power / ability / life / knowledge and other desirable qualities. These values are ingrained within the soul and are beamed at the self.

The higher meaning of events and situations become more evident with the development of the intellect and reason, as personal consciousness accesses soul consciousness. Physical and emotional concerns of earlier years begin to be displaced by the quest for meaning, relating to the nature of the psyche, death, self-knowledge and enlightenment. The yearning for inner contentment and happiness takes precedence over outer drives, pleasures and acquisition. Spiritual wisdom and evolvement will enable the seeker to catch glimpses of the immensity within the moment and perfections flashed upon the screen of the present.

The less one has concern for outer actions, the greater the possibilities for inner awakening.

The physical or tangible aspect of the self comprises numerous levels of discernable as well as other delicate systems, transmissions and receptions beyond measurements and control. The physical and structural part of the human self is an amazingly complex body with its multitudes of dynamically interactive organs and faculties. The mind is the seat of connecting and interpreting inner and outer senses and emotions backed by memories, experiences and values, which are ordered according to a changing hierarchy of perceived needs.

The need to belong, to be secure, acknowledged, loved and regarded by others as considered special are all desired by the self, for it seeks to emulate the soul.

The inner heart is a precious faculty and requires serious attention, care and purification for it to be the meeting ground between self and soul. Otherwise, the self remains restless, confused and hopelessly seeking affirmation from its own ego. This perversion is the root of depression, anger, sorrow, grief, hate, madness and other negative tendencies. The ego is a product of the mind, memories and other experiences of conditioned consciousness. The ego arises when the self identifies with different roles, values or images and is not experiencing regular recharging from higher consciousness.

We are creatures of habit and hence it is a natural human tendency to care for what is already known, thus the inner heart remains neglected, undiscovered and undernourished.

Human emotions are learned and acquired naturally; as one grows they come under the control of self awareness to varying degrees. They include the positive and the negative, and all that is in between. The negative emotions can be superseded by the rational mind, whereas the positive emotions will help in the growth of the self towards its evolvement and illumination. The influence of emotions weakens as the rational mind grows stronger and the intellect dominates the thinking process, whilst the heart is still referred to. This state relates to spiritual intelligence.

When the self is spiritually evolved, it spontaneously turns away from unethical behaviour as the intellect resonates with the soul's perfections.

Normally in a healthy person the body, mind and heart interact and evaluate the appropriate responses to a situation, in order to restore balance and equilibrium between the person and the outer world. The evolved seeker realises that every disease brings with it the latent power of healing and learning, if the heart and soul are referred to. God gives the answers to whoever calls upon him sincerely and relies on him. The supreme light of divine consciousness is always there and we can tap into it. Blessings and curses are never separate from each other and what is required is the optimum understanding within the appropriate context. There are, on occasion, processes that are not reversible or a disease that is not curable. However, there is compensation in every situation which often more than makes up for the handicap.

Gold is purified by blazing fire and the self by worldly affliction and constriction.

The spiritual imprints and transmissions of the soul resonate through the human heart, affecting the person's body, mind, intellect and all levels of being. Illness and disease occur when alignments and connections are faulty or out of harmony. Wholesomeness implies unity between a healthy body, a sound mind, a sharp intellect and a pure heart.

With desires and attachments you are often misled; yet without them you are lifeless. Thus have the one desire worth living for: unity of consciousnesses.

The mysterious composition of self and soul within humankind – with its outer/inner, meaning/form and other polarities – reproduce and reflect a mirror image of all that is in the outer earthly world and the heavens. The soul draws its light from the divine, unseen realm and in turn it energises all the physical and subtler components of the whole person. The soul is the partner of the self in an irrevocable fashion in this world and the next, but this reality needs to be understood, realised and experienced by each person. This is the challenge of discovering how the outer and inner worlds meet and complement each other within the human heart – that most precious entity, yet perhaps the least cared for!

Memory reinforces self identity and the illusion of free will and control. This conditioned consciousness fades in the light of higher consciousness – just as the stars disappear when the sun shines.

A constant challenge for human beings to resolve is the drive and desire for lasting contentment and inner peace. This state can be experienced when the self is least encumbered by egoistical concerns and focuses upon the inner heart. A fulfilled life is the result of a healthy mind and purified heart, which guide the self. If the human being neglects this most important task then mental confusion and distress will naturally predominate. This prevailing sickness will cause both the individual, as well as society, to pay the price of negligence in blood and chaos. This tragic situation is sometimes blamed upon divine punishment or other supernatural reasons. It is our own neglect and wrong actions that generate human afflictions and sufferings which are warning signs for a return to reunion between head and heart.

Under light one can see and discriminate with clarity. In darkness confusion and loss prevail with regrettable consequences.

The soul is god's favourite creation. The self, too, desires to be god's chosen one. In fact, every entity in creation sees itself as the centre of existence. All human beings are god's chosen and are equal in potential but differ according to actual spiritual evolvement. Creation and life are the overflow of divine cosmic consciousness from which the soul draws its life force. However, when life is conceived in the womb, soul consciousness activates the self and energises it with personal consciousness. These two different levels of consciousness relate and complement each other as the person grows up in the world. Unity in consciousness is the ultimate goal in life and the foundation of fulfilment.

Every form, state or feeling experienced by the self has its meaning and pattern within the human soul. A biography is the specific unfoldment of the personal journey from pure (innocent) light of childhood to the all-encompassing light of divine presence.

The human challenge is to understand and accept the world of duality and constant outer change, whilst interacting appropriately with attention and desire for overall harmony and wellbeing. Consistent success in this endeavour is not achievable. Nevertheless, the self continues the quest for excellence so long as it is in the confines of the world of space-time. The self has no option other than to carry on interacting with various outcomes, whilst referring to the heart for guidance, inspiration and affirmation. Human love for exploration and discovery is part of the self's response to the call of the soul to be good.

Human needs stimulate the self towards seeking fulfilment and contentment which is always present but often not realised due to distractions and egotistic expectations.

The paradigms of holograms and mirrors are helpful in understanding the relationship between the self and soul. The soul is like an authentic holographic image of the universal soul or god. It contains the knowledge and patterns of archetypes, all the energy fields and whatever there is in creation. The soul beams its light upon the self and produces a semi-holographic image, which needs development and spiritual growth in order to perfect its intended destiny. The self also acts like a mirror with a dark side, which is the ego. It is on this side that human vices erupt into undesirable conduct when the self is confused and not aligned with the perfect soul.

At the lowest end of the self, the egotistic mind acts like a black-hole with high entropy or chaos. At the highest end, the self takes on the beautiful colours of the soul.

If the self turns away from the dark egotistic 'self image' and faces the soul it resonates with wholesomeness. Then its 'soul image hologram' matches the perfect soul. This is like the full moon reflecting the light of the sun maximally. The extreme opposite occurs when the self's mirror has turned away from the soul and is cut off from its light. Usually, most selves swing on a pivot, sometimes reflecting the soul and its clarity, other times being sucked into the black hole of the ego. The struggle in human life is to educate the self. The root meaning of educate is to draw out and align it with the soul's consciousness.

The self seeks instant gratification, avoids being caught with wrong action, and wishes to be acknowledged, to excel, to be independent, to be secure and content. All these qualities are emitted by the soul and can be accessed by the subdued self.

Self, in relation to soul, is like a prodigal child with a loving, accepting and patient parent. The soul knows that the self is obsessed and addicted to the body and its mental biography and is patiently awaiting for the self to grow, evolve and be weaned of this condition. In the meantime, the self is preoccupied with the survival and care of the body so as to reduce the agitations of the mind and other lifelong habits and concerns.

When the self submits to its soul it is released from worldly tension and enters communion with higher consciousness and opens windows onto spiritual vistas.

Although the human paradox will not be solved by the mind, it will dissolve with the correct intention, diligent action and spiritual knowledge. The outcome of this will be witnessing existence 'as it is', and taking delight in all perfections reflected in the eternal sacred moment which connects heaven and earth.

Life's great puzzle is that everything in creation is based on duality whose root and essence is unity. The human paradox is even more subtle in that personal consciousness reflects creational duality, whilst soul consciousness represents unity. The resolution of this mystery occurs when consciousness is united in the heart.

2.3. UNITY

Only when you are one (consistently within yourself) can you begin to know the one and only ONE.

All of creation has emanated from one unique universal essence which originates, permeates, energises, organises and controls all that exists within space-time and beyond. The fabric of existence is made up of interconnected energy fields in constant dynamic flux, criss-crossed by electromagnetic forces, chemical and physical reactions and multitudes of other interactive systems. What appears to be chaotic from one viewpoint has its own intrinsic perfect order when looked at from a higher angle. A spontaneous forest fire may be seen as disastrous to a nearby human settlement but it rejuvenates vegetation and is necessary for seed germination. When human vision is refocused beyond the immediate concerns regarding the event or fact, it will witness aspects of perfection not noticed before.

Divinity is never separate from humanity. In fact, it is the divine light that creates and sustains all of creation. It is ever present within creation and beyond.

Unity and singularity is the root and foundation of all dualities. Life spans a spectrum of movement and consciousness along multiple polarities and complementary opposites. The cosmic light is the unique self-sustaining eternal light and power upon which all multiplicities depend and from which they draw their life's energy and patterns. This is the meaning of absolute divine oneness or truth. The more you reflect upon the one essence behind diverse creations, the more you see harmony and complementarity in what appears to be conflicting opposites. The universal soul and one essence is veiled behind flickering creational manifestations. Upon this cosmic screen countless earthly and heavenly images, energies and entities appear and disappear. Sight helps us in the world of multiplicities and insight with the light of unity. Sight discerns rainbows and shadows while insight discerns pure light and its variations.

The universal soul is the only source and container of all creation. In the world of dispersion, all beings seek the original security of gatheredness in the ONE.

Experiences and relationships within creation can only be fully understood with reference to the essence from whence they emanated. Thus, every event or experience has within it the light of perfection in essence, which has given it its patterns and identity. The natural human quest and search is the outer response of the inner call of the soul. The self is ever-restless whilst the soul is ever-peaceful and content. The self desires fulfilment, whilst the soul is always fulfilled.

The personal source of human life and consciousness is the soul, which energises the self, body, mind and heart.

The soul's purpose is to bring together in harmony the diverse physical and subtle entities within us. Childish consciousness starts with worldly discernment and evolves towards meanings, insights and higher consciousness. The heart is the reception hall for the meeting between the self and the soul. When the heart is pure and receptive, then it is a fitting wedding chamber for the union of consciousness. The supreme cosmic consciousness or god's light prevails with boundless grace.

Every entity in existence is designed to realise its full potential with natural ease. This is the highest level a particular consciousness can reach.

Throughout human history, thinkers, philosophers, prophets and scientists have recognised the need for a reliable reference point or truth to which to relate human ideas, visions, wisdom and theories. Space and time were considered absolute until the advent of quantum physics with its definition of a field of universal connectivity outside the realm of cause and effect and natural worldly laws. It is the human mental perception of separation and distance in time and space that drives us towards deeper exploration and search for meaning and purpose in life. Multiplicity causes the illusion of the many different and independent entities and thus veils the original essence of unity and gatheredness, which is present within all and at all times. All human endeavours aim to gain this unifying lens so as to realise the perfect cosmic connections.

The world of dualities, complementarities and symmetries are relative entities rooted in the truth of absolute unity. In essence there is only one and it is due to that root of unity that differences and separation appear.

When outer and inner consciousness are in harmony deep contentment prevails. Like light, which is both photon and wave, a human being is a tangible entity, (body and self) as well as energy (soul) not confined to space-time. Specific events and responses change and condition the self, whereas the soul is not directly affected by events. The ultimate stage of human evolution and maturity occurs when the person's mind, emotions, intellect, heart and soul interact harmoniously.

The path towards unity begins with bringing about harmony in body, mind, heart and soul and that is optimum relationship between the microcosm and macrocosm.

Cosmic consciousness is the source and root of all levels of consciousness; pure, modified, reflected, conditioned, narrow, weak and intense. The self seeks higher consciousness and the qualities radiated from the soul. The self, at best, can attain temporarily and partially these qualities. Its dependency upon the soul is like the earth with the sun: life on earth will cease without the sun. The self is the prodigal son of the soul and is always accepted and loved by it unconditionally. When the self surrenders fully to the soul's mastery and supremacy, authentic peace will prevail.

Recognition and acceptance of the self's dependence upon the soul is the door to the realisation that god is the supreme source and sustaining power of all souls.

The self, with its body, senses, mind, intellect and other faculties connects the earthly, tangible world with the soul's domain of higher consciousness via the heart. The purified heart is the junction between earth and heavens and it is where the soul is centred. For this reason a pure heart overflowing with love and compassion is essential for spiritual awakening. Most religious and spiritual practices, ethics and moral rules are attempts to purify the heart. Most religious restrictions and laws are there to make the self accept boundaries in the hope of conscious connectedness with the boundless soul.

Love at all its levels is the divine glue that binds together creation in the world and unifies diversity. Hate is the absence of love and signifies dispersion and loss.

As everything in existence is balanced between two complementary opposites, every human experience takes place on two levels, each requiring a different attitude and approach. Seeking the root of duality will activate the golden thread of unity, which is the foundation of all consciousnesses. Turn away from twos in order to witness one. Life's experiences flow through the umbilical cord of unity to energise all dualities and diversities in creation. The process of striving to witness this perfection is spiritual progress and growth.

The numerous personalities and moods and minds in you will make sense when seen through the unifying lens of the heart.

In the material world patterns and natural laws maintain outer balance, harmony and equilibrium. The laws of the heavenly domain and the sub-atomic world are fundamentally different to our so-called 'normal' or 'real' world. An entirely different logic prevails in these domains. The outer earthly world requires a clear mind, sharp intellect, heightened rationality and discipline. The door to higher consciousness and what is beyond the world of space-time is through a pure heart and is illumined by the soul. Such a world does not follow the same mathematical precision or symmetry of the earthly world.

Duality and plurality are only short-lived manifestations of the one unique eternal light. By contemplation and 'insight' one can discern the ever-present light behind all its shadows.

Personal human experiences on this earth are bracketed between birth and death. They are samples and windows to what is beyond our world of space-time. Our life on earth has some similarities to the state of the hereafter. The baby emerges mysteriously from the womb and drifts into the world of cause and effect, emotions and rationality. Then the mature self moves towards higher realms of consciousness and the unseen in preparation for departure to the hereafter. In this birth, the self acts as a shroud over the soul accompanying it on its ongoing journey. The hereafter is where the self knows the truth but is unable to act, whereas in this world it can act but with only limited knowledge.

What you consider far is near and that which you think is near is distant. Truth is neither near nor far as such. It is not subject to space or time. It is just there: permanent and absolute.

The omnipresent oneness encompasses the whole cosmos but is veiled by the appearance of dualities and the accompanying distraction of separation and individuality. Whatever is above is represented below (and vice versa). This is how the miracle of one manifests in the multitude. The physical world is not separate from the spiritual except in outer appearance and predominance. All colours are conditioned light but appear with different qualities and identities.

The sacred light of divine unity binds what appears as earthly diversities.

The outer connection or union we seek is a small attempt to reproduce the intrinsic unifying power within all of creation. The truth is that there is one primary source, cause and essence for all existence and creation. The whole universe is the visible overflowing of lights and attributes of the one creator, sustainer, ever-present master and lord of all. That divine essence contains all and everything contains its traces and signs.

Lovers become most anxious the closer they are to reunion. The nearer you are to your soul, the more you become impatient with the old habit of feeling separate.

2.4. TRUTH AND REALITIES

Truth is timeless, boundless and eternal. It is beyond all perception and yet it is the root of perception. Everything relates to truth and reflects an aspect of it. Truth is like a beam from cosmic consciousness that affects all other levels of consciousness.

For centuries philosophers and scientists have discussed, postulated and wondered about the rules that govern the universe. There are two distinctly different sets of laws: one set which describes phenomena like gravity (general relativity) and deals with the everyday physical world, and another called quantum mechanics which describes the small fundamental particles which are at the root of the material world. A number of theories and ideas have been developed by physicists that attempt to unify these two different set of laws. Most of these get stuck at defining the role of space and time in the drama of life. Is matter some form of modification of space-time or is space-time an unchanging grid or structure?

The human being represents the ultimate fusion between the finite and infinite as actually experienced by the two spheres of consciousness — the conditioned personal and the higher or soul consciousness. We are the locus of the earth and heavens and the unifier of the discernable physical world of general relativity and the subatomic world. The human heart has already been molded by this strange cosmic elixir to comprehend the two domains and yet feel intact as one being.

The answer to this most perplexing issue is nearer at hand then we think because it is ingrained within the human psyche. Our actual human experience seems to span both realms of general relativity as well as the quantum field. The physical, material and tangible aspect of the human being seems to reflect and complement the illusive inner world which is not subject to the rules of space and time. One domain seems to be logical, rational and can be related to our minds, whilst the other seems to echo the vast possibilities of our inner heart.

With deeper reflection we can understand that the human consciousness encompasses both of these realms and the meeting point of their unity is the awakened heart where self (relative) and soul (quantum) unite at peace and reflect the interactivity of energy and matter.

Happiness is the outcome of the self being constant in its synchrony with the soul. It is a by product of unity at heart.

We experience life in relative terms and according to relationships within time and space. Faster or slower, better or worse, happy or happier, content or frustrated: each relates to the other with varying degrees. Every entity, emotion or thought is in relation to something of its kind or opposite in nature. The human soul is inherently attuned to its origin in supreme consciousness and the higher qualities and perfections. Thus, the soul is the ultimate reference point within us and is centred within the inner heart.

Truth relates to absolute knowledge and to the power of the creator that connects and energises all creation.

Truth is the perfect reference point for any reality. The soul reflects the truth of god's supremacy and omnipresence. Truth is the constant, ever-present calibrator and measurer of all realities. Truth is not subject to space-time limitations, for it permeates everything that is discernable and beyond. Every image or state appears as real; the longer its duration the greater the perception that it is indeed real or true. Repetition, habit, common human acceptance, appreciation, understanding and sharing of common values, strengthen the illusion of outer worldly realities. Without memory the outer world will not assume its durability. Without past recollection our present world would seem amorphous, foggy and unreal.

The constancy and permanency of truth is veiled by ever-changing realities and experiences, which appear like flickering images upon the screen of truth.

Truth is permanent and self-revealing through diverse realities, which appear in a specific location or for limited durations. Every reality has a limited life span and extent of influence within space-time. Wisdom is to evaluate a reality by its influence and life span, which determines the extent of its closeness to truth. Thus, the further a reality is from truth, the less durable or 'true' it is. The greater the illusion, the further it is away from the truth. A lie can be closer to truth than what is normally considered as real, for a lie does not pretend to be true, whilst what is not a clear lie or deception may pretend to be true, which cannot be so because truth is permanent and absolute. In truth, there is only truth and everything else is an approximate (or a lie) to varying degrees. Whatever moves or changes is a transient reality and at best only carries a trace of the light of truth.

Pure light is absolute. All other lights are conditioned and compromised in comparison to the original light. Everything in creation has only a shade of truth within in.

Generosity is an appropriate act in a given situation. It can be measured and evaluated in quality and quantity according to its closeness or distance from the best generous act. Perfect generosity is an aspect of truth and brings about perfect harmony, equilibrium and total contentment in its time. True generosity is a quality within the soul, which the self manifests in the relative worldly setting. The absolute can only be discerned briefly by the relative.

The wisdom of doing unto others as you would have done to yourself is an attempt to bring about sameness to otherness. In truth there is only one essence from which everything in creation draws its life force.

The hierarchy of realities is based on their repeatability, durability and impact upon the self. The longer a reality persists in time, the closer it is to the truth. A toothache is real, so is the need for shelter, but when the toothache is cured it is forgotten, while the need for shelter is more durable and thus more true. We are all travellers on different roads and highways of realities, surrounded by ever changing scenery and climates. What drives us on is the inner urge to explore and discover the root, essence and constant truth behind all these phenomena and experiences. We all need and seek durable meaning and purpose in life, as we evolve towards the ever present perfect truth. The light of truth within the soul is the instigator and energiser of the human quest from beginning to end.

Truth is unbounded and all other realities are limited and defined reflections of it within space-time. Truth is beyond space and time and yet flashes within all domains.

Differentiation, distinction and specific identifications appear real when the mind's imaginal faculty relates to different entities and energies. All creations, states and patterns in existence interact with and impact upon each other in different levels of order or strength. Every experienced state of reality is related in some measure, either weakly or strongly, to the truth and accordingly is given an order of importance by the experiencer. The self cannot be fully content with relativities unless it relates these to the permanent truth within. Indeed, most people will readily reveal their dissatisfaction, insecurity or unhappiness when given a chance to step out of polite composure. An honest person will confess to having doubts or hopes regarding arrival at truth and spiritual wisdom.

Our search for permanent security, inner peace and contentment relates to eternal truth and not to temporary worldly states.

The world of change becomes manageable and meaningful by referring it to the soul's state of stability. The relative can only make sense and be dealt with appropriately in reference to the absolute. Thus, the meaning or purpose of life on earth can be read and understood through the heavenly language of heart and soul. The outer announces what is within the inner with aspects of meaning, essence and truth. Similarly, body language reveals what verbal language has modified or left unmentioned. The threads of interconnection in creation are vertical, horizontal, as well as multi-directional and multi-dimensional.

What we consider as rational is never fixed or permanent. The root of the word is ratio, which is a relative measurement. Spiritual intelligence is at the peak of the intellect and close to truth.

The human desire to speed up time and events to achieve an outer goal is rooted in the self's impatience with the temporal world as it seeks permanent contentment and peace. A wise person is patient with other creations and worldly situations but impatient with his own unawakened self. The truth is not subject to time, whereas all worldly realities are. By itself the mind cannot grasp the truth but it can take a first step towards it by looking towards the heart.

Every aspect of the observable world appears as finite although its essence and root is boundless and eternal.

Truth resides within the human heart, whereas all changing realities are outer manifestations projected upon truth. The truth is always thinly veiled behind a lie; for example, a photograph is a lie depicting a glimpse of truth. Your picture was a true reflection of your image at the time it was taken but is no longer. A lie is that which is not constant, while truth is ever the same. The supreme truth is that *all contains all* and *everything relates to everything.*

Facts are real but change or disappear with time. Truth is eternally constant as it is not subject to time and space and it is absolutely independent.

You can never define or study truth for it encompasses every manifestation in life including our contemplation of it. Truth is part of us and we need to refer to it constantly in order to balance our inner and outer states. Pure consciousness of the soul is an aspect of truth close at hand. Look with the eye of the soul at falsehood and transient realities and the self will be enlivened by its enlarged consciousness. We know the permanent through the transitory and perfection through the imperfect, god through creation, heavens through the earth.

Within all chaos and confusion lies the essence of truth, which is perfect order and harmony with different contextual backdrops.

The human self naturally and consistently applies double standards (bias towards itself) until it has unified with its own soul and perceives through the lens of unity. The self operates in the world of duality and opposites; the soul is in the abode of oneness. On earth, justice is always relative; in the heavens it is absolute. The self is worldly and the soul is heavenly, hence the human struggle is to apply heavenly justice in a relative and ever-changing world. This dynamic will be in balance when the soul rules our self and ego.

A conservative seeks reality by repeating the past; a revolutionary seeks continuity by changing the past. Both attempts to experience the ever-constant truth appearing as ever-changing.

Information and facts are news and views, varying in accuracy and relevancy; whereas knowledge and wisdom relate to appropriateness, which bring about desirable results. For wisdom you need reason, logic and rational deduction, a cool head and a warm heart. To know truth you need intuition, a pure heart and higher consciousness. It is perfectly in order, for instance, to compromise with some existential matters and with most outer aspects in life. Wisdom grows when the powers of attraction and repulsion are harnessed through exercising courage, modesty, justice and wisdom. This quadrangle is a necessary foundation for clear witnessing, understanding and harmonious relationships in life. The emerging reason and rationality will lead to inner realisation of truth. By reason alone you will not know truth and without reason you will remain in confused ignorance.

Truth predominates when falsehood is denied. Truth is the cause of all changing realities and experiences, which depend upon it.

Spiritual knowledge refers to insights, meanings and essence, which highlight the truth behind a situation. When you are at sea and your position is obscure, you use the stars, the horizon, a compass or global positioning system as a reference and apply this knowledge to your direction. The success of your voyage depends upon the accuracy of the reference you have taken and your skill at navigation. Whatever you experience in life has a reality with varying degrees of durability and the longer lasting ones are closer to truth. We consider anything short-lived to be less real than what is more durable. Hunger is a reality when you have abstained from food but no longer exists after eating a meal. Seeking happiness is a reality that always persists and as such it smacks of truth. A dream can sometimes reveal more truth than a worldly event. Every experience, occurrence or event contains an aspect of truth. Even a lie has a relationship with truth: it is what truth is not.

Truth differs from all other realities with regards to durability and persistence. Truth is always true. A reality will bear an aspect of truth in a specific context and time only.

An evolving self remains uncertain until it resonates with its soul. Rebellion is part of the nature of the self and freedom remains an illusion until until the self surrenders to the soul. Hence, awareness of the ever-changing experiences of the self or ego and the realisation of the ever constancy and reliability of the soul, as a reference point, is the objective of the seeker. Each person needs to recognise and work at and transcend their particular personal veils and barriers of false 'self-hood'.

The self hides its ignorance (otherwise it will lose the illusion of its identity) whilst the soul broadcasts its knowledge. The self needs acknowledgment and the soul knows it is acknowledged.

During youth it is natural and healthy for the self to be egocentric, to seek self-images, expressing a strong personality and desiring to be loved and acknowledged by others. The self likes to be described as beautiful and intelligent. The soul knows it *is* beauty and intelligence. The wise and mature adult is less concerned about the ego or emotional affirmation by others and lives more fully aware of the present moment, free from outer illusions, whilst seeking perfection in the light of presence. Salvation is when desire for worldly success and power are superseded by spiritual knowledge and delight.

When you witness perfection in an event or situation, irrespective of its desirability or otherwise, then you are on the threshold of truth. The perfect moment is beyond good or bad.

Every move and incentive in life is powered by passion and love for the intrinsic unseen quality within the soul which beckon the self to them. What the person seeks is a reliable focal point or anchor, which prevents the self from being distracted by the outer concerns or egotistic pitfalls. A person in love with another feels both good and bad. Human love affairs are only an elusive reflection of the primal passion instilled in the self to seek its soul. All worldly loves are temporary or poor reproductions of the primal divine love for the soul and that of the soul for its protégé: the self. Self concern or selfishness is reduced and love and care for others is increased when a person is in love with another person or absorbed in serving a higher cause. Love reduces darkness and enhances the light from heart.

Love is the fuel of life and all of creation draws energy from it and follows along its channels, including the powers of attraction and repulsion.

Love is the primal foundation for the interchange and exchange of all the energy fields in creation. It is the power that drives us towards stability and contentment, which is the original state in creation. The ultimate and crucial desire of the serious seeker is freedom from all outer material loves and desires. The state we aspire to is inner passion for increased awareness and unity in consciousness. For the contemplative seeker, ordinary love and desires are the first step towards passion for the truth whose beam of light is transmitted through the soul, reflecting god's call to cosmic oneness.

The power of love drives every entity to evolve towards its ultimate potential. Primal love is nature's force, which drives creation at the beginning, in the middle and at the end.

We experience love's numerous levels and qualities through our feelings and senses, culminating in passion beyond reason for the eternal perfect state. Divine love is what holds the universe together within the unified cosmic web. In the final stage of passionate love, the lover's identity and the notion of separation between the loving self and the beloved soul is lost. This state is referred to as god intoxication, gnosis, annihilation and enlightenment. The light is blindingly effulgent and is mercifully veiled by layers of reflections, deflections and modifications, experienced as attributes and qualities desired and aspired for by us. Love of a quality, or a thing or person, is the first step on the ladder of higher consciousness, culminating with boundless and timeless passion for the heavenly truth.

Truth encompasses what we consider to be natural, as well as what is regarded as unnatural or miraculous. In truth there is only truth. In truth it is only God in existence.

Love is behind the drive of every endeavour. It motivates the desire to satisfy all real or imagined needs. Love of a companion aims to draw together complementary attributes to experience some stability and wellbeing. Love constantly drives us towards excellence and perfection in all things. Thus, divine love is behind all love so that we come to see only eternal perfections, after having lost ourselves in the all-consuming passion for the omnipotent source of all creation.

Truth reveals itself in levels and degrees and overrides what was considered to be real.

In truth, there is only truth in all of existence; everything else is its shadow. There is no god but god. Those who are illumined see truth in every moment, for every flicker betrays an aspect of the everlasting truth. Original love has emanated from the eternal truth and is its agent of cosmic oneness. This heavenly love affair is the source of every other love, which emanates from minds and hearts. 'God was a hidden treasure and loved to be known and thus he created.'

All realities, states, experiences, as well as illusions are held together by one everlasting absolute truth, transmitting numerous levels of love: one divine light giving rise to countless lights, colours and shadows within space-time and beyond.

3. THE EVOLVING SELF

Every human soul contains the essence of all creation and their meaning. The individual self evolves in consciousness as it experiences creational events and aspires towards the soul's perfection and its freedom from space-time limitations.

When self and soul unite at heart, a person experiences a degree of wholeness and contentment in life. The soul transmits pure consciousness and multitudes of admirable attributes, giving hope and purpose to the self. The self of every being is different — specific — and evolves towards the soul. Personal consciousness and the state of body, mind and heart, grow and evolve through life's experiences towards the soul and higher consciousness. The groomed and mature self submits to the soul and experiences unison and contentment.

Birth, growth, maturity and death are all activities relating to the self and its material identification along the journey, which starts with one cell growing into a most complex human being. Upon death the self departs from the physical world along with the soul. The evolving self experiences diverse states until it attains the soul's universal essence. The self's enlightenment comes with the recognition of its total dependence on, adoration and love of the soul and its creator; the unique everlasting one, who can only be known through his great qualities and created dualities.

The achievement of harmonious alignment between self and soul is the ultimate purpose of human life. The journey begins with the self's identification with the body and mind and ends in its union at heart with its soul.

The self always seeks stimulus, thrill and new discoveries which are all superseded by increased awareness of the perfect moment.

3.1. STEPPING STONES

The power of consciousness drives the self to seek its desired destiny, which is in the abode of the heart where the soul is centred.

Discovering and understanding the fabric of existence has been a great challenge to all thinkers, philosophers, sages and scientists throughout the ages. The desire for exploration and discovery is a primal drive for human beings to prepare for the future in order to survive, grow and procreate. The soul is forever alive and blissful, while its protégé (the self) seeks its qualities by choice and actions. This process is guided by feedback from the senses, mind, intellect, heart and soul.

The soul is the faithful divine representative within the human heart, whose work is fulfilled when its outer shadow, the self, recognises its source of life and submits to it.

Life's earliest signs appeared several hundred million years ago with the act of cellular duplication. The blue-green algae and protoplasm heralded the earliest primitive living forms. With energy from sunlight, hydrocarbon molecules were formed and photosynthesis enabled the single-cell plants (or single-cell animal) to be sustained and multiply. It is the combination of individuality, the boundary of a cell and light (cosmic rays) that is the earthly origin of mankind on earth. Evolution culminated in the emergence of the human with a soul that contains the imprint of all that is in existence, including the big bang and other earthly and cosmic events. The human kingdom of body, mind, heart and soul is a microcosm of the world's macrocosm. The human soul is a sacred hologram, which reproduces all the divine qualities, attributes and designs in existence. It is the combination of pure consciousness and conditioned personal consciousness that is unique to human beings.

Every entity in creation asserts its presence and broadcasts its nature whilst evolving towards its highest potential state.

Evolution is a natural occurrence in the world of space-time. In this realm we experience causality and numerous links in chains of events. It appears that from non-existence all of creation has emerged and a time will come (probably after a few billion years) when everything returns, or is submerged back into that incomprehensible 'nothingness.' Natural selection is quite natural but also, like other normal or natural events, contains aspects of supra-natural and inexplicable mysteries. The human soul and consciousness is one such major inexplicable entity. The human soul contains in essence all patterns and designs, quantitatively and qualitatively, of whatever there is in creation. Thus, the human soul represents the most perplexing paradox that 'one contains all' and 'all is in one'.

'You presume that you are a small entity, whereas within you is enfolded the entire universe.'

The soul's throne and command centre is the inner heart, where it connects through the rational mind to the body, mind and self. Human wellbeing depends on the extent of the self's connectedness with the soul and the resonance between personal consciousness and soul consciousness. The journey of the self is for the purpose of learning how to listen, submit and be led by the soul, which is god's resident agent, representative and witness.

Moving from lower primal consciousness to soul consciousness is a subtle and continuous process of displacement. Less of one is more of the other.

The consciousness of a baby is simple, limited, and relates to basic survival needs and vegetative and animalistic growth. However, soon the baby develops in reasoning and intelligence. The outer senses activate and develop the mind's memory by connecting millions of brain cells into complex circuits and data banks, which are sorted by categories of importance and access. The early experiences and awareness of the outer world lead towards emotional growth of the self and egocentricity. A child's reliance and respect for parents is essential in learning to trust and love others and this ultimately leads to following the voice of the heart. Spiritual intelligence and transformation occur when personal consciousness is attuned to pure consciousness within the soul and unifies with it.

A child needs routine and continuity whilst widening relationships and connections. A grown-up needs to break outer norms and routine. The self of a child needs to grow with confidence and selfishness. An adult's self needs modesty, courage, wisdom and unison with the soul.

Every person at every moment in life is an identifiable entity with unique biological features, anatomical systems and other characteristics, which make up the whole being. Beside the five outer senses there are five inner senses, which include the imaginal faculty and the associated mental values (perception without sensation) given to events and experiences. This faculty of imagination expands and evolves the mind and gives consciousness the perception and definition of forms and boundaries. Our physical outer world is as such an 'imaginal' solid world. The whole person is made up of physiological, psychological and biological systems, as well as electromagnetic, biochemical and numerous other energy systems and patterns, all are interlinked through the inner heart and energised by the soul.

A clear, rational mind is a prelude for the disciplined self to gain access to the purified heart and the light of the soul therein.

The mind starts with emotions and evolves towards reason, rationality, intellect and beyond. Selfishness, like many other vices, is rooted in the need to preserve the self/ego as it grows and evolves towards its intended destiny of selflessness and transcendence. The enlightened self perceives the world through the lens of the soul. This ultimate state of wholesomeness is the result of unity between conditioned consciousness and pure consciousness. The spring and fountainhead of this life force is the soul, which is ever-connected to the supreme cosmic consciousness.

Every moment in life is different from the previous one. Yet the self experiences continuity, which is a light transmitted from the ever-constant soul.

For the seeker of truth, every experience is a stepping-stone towards a better understanding of the meanings behind specific events. Eventually, all meanings converge on the divine field of perfect attributes and qualities emanating from one essence. At one end of the spectrum, events seem diverse and different from each other, whereas at the other end they unite and meet at the root. At the outer visible end, there is distinct separation and differentiation, whereas in essence there is singularity and unity. This is how opposite qualities balance and unite. This is how diverse energies and forms emerge, grow and return back to source.

The extent of your engagement with worldly activities and attachment to your projects describe the condition of your inner state. Your relationships are a good indicator of your condition.

The human cycle of birth and death is like an echo of the cosmic inception, expansion, evolution and ultimate return to the original nothingness. The journey from light, back to it and by it, is reflected at many levels in the outer world, as well as within us. From the moment of conception in the womb the human journey is energised by the soul's consciousness. The journey follows a path of outer separation whilst the self yearns for the original unity. The religious reference of returning to the lord of creation is imprinted in the soul of every individual being and is reflected in human behaviour, consciously or otherwise. The evolving self needs to merge back into the soul through the doorway of the heart to confirm the intended destiny of unification in form and meaning.

Life's journey is like a walk through a cavernous tunnel with flashing lights, mirrors and images. The navigational aids needed are the rational clear mind and the pure heart.

Stepping-stones in life take us from the egotistic state of outer concerns to the delights of pure consciousness. The evolvement of a child to a mature adult is a complex process of numerous steps and stages of growth and change. Initially the physical dimension of experience occupies prominence in childhood. Then mental and emotional growth leads to the development of reasoning and subtler awareness relating to spiritual maturity. While a child's concern is mostly with the physical and emotional, a mature person has evolved to the rational and subtler levels of consciousness. During our growth we traverse multitudes of levels in form and meaning, both outwardly and inwardly. A successful seeker is one whose focus has changed from form to meaning and from the mind to the heart and from shadows and lights.

When a snake has outgrown its outer skin, it wriggles out of it and leaves it behind. We too sometimes need a major outer change by migrating to a new situation, or changing profession, life style, environment or country of residence.

The stepping-stones of life take us from primordial slush to the heavenly abode of perfection both literally and figuratively. These designs and steps are etched upon the soul of the human being and are enacted by the individual self. The baby begins to grow by developing a mind and making sense of the world around it. The mature and wise person learns to read subtle meanings for the unseen world of heartfelt truth. A serious seeker tries to understand the meaning and purpose of life. An enlightened person has overcome fear of death by understanding the nature of the afterlife through knowing the eternal soul within the heart.

The self's concerns change from basic physical care towards subtler understandings. Love for meanings and knowledge will replace basic early desires.

Human intentions and actions leave their traces and inner records by affecting one's personality and human behaviour. After death the person will re-live the final state of the overall consciousness it has attained. The hereafter will be experienced through the background life of the 'here'. Hell 'there' is an extension of having lived in confusion and chaos 'here'. The heavenly garden is being cultivated and planted by our intentions and actions 'here'. This garden comes to full bloom with the spiritual union of the self and soul in the heart's palace. This secret garden emits heavenly perfumes, metaphysically and materially.

For a novice mountaineer at the base of the mountain the steps are easy and falls not fatal. Near the top you need an experienced guide, for there a wrong step could be a major disaster.

Human growth in outer knowledge and wisdom is a prelude to inner knowledge, wisdom and perfection. This truth energises and sustains the world and all of its lights and shadows. Thus, every move and change in life is a step towards realising the perfect soul consciousness within us, which is the cause and the motivation of the search in the first place. The journey and evolvement in life is about witnessing perfection and attaining sustainable contentment. The experiences of a disciplined seeker following a path of transformation in this life is like a joyful walk along stepping-stones in earthly gardens, which replicate heavenly designs. Each step is different; all carry the hallmark of full awareness, self control and reference to the map within the heart, where earth and heavens are in unison.

The spiritual journey starts with much 'self'-consciousness of the body, senses and the outer world. Then inner awareness grows with the discovery of soul consciousness within the heart. From now on, the spiritual compass is the guide in one's life.

3.2. PERSONALITY AND CHARACTER

Every thought, move or action will either get you closer to your heart and soul or further away towards the ego's shadows of falsehood and illusions.

The human soul transmits its qualities to the self at every stage of growth and evolvement. The soul contains both male and female principles, thus it is in unison and balance; in the self, however, one or the other gender usually dominates. A personality at any moment in time is the cumulative outcome of interaction between the body, mind, emotions, memories, rationality, society, culture and other factors. A person's behaviour reflects the state of the self, especially the mind and its subtle chemistry and the extent of spiritual evolvement. A neurotic or maladjusted person with clusters of negative traits will behave in a discordant and confused manner reflecting their inner state.

The ego will often stubbornly persist with its waywardness unless consistent reminders from outside and within subdue it.

A character is never a fixed entity for it is the outcome of interactive factors and influences. Personal consciousness is mostly based upon the ego, emotions, reasons, rationality and other layers of voluntary and involuntary recalls of memories, as well as the autonomic nervous system. The quality of a character relates to the state of the health and relationships of body, mind, heart and soul. A selfish thought looks at a situation exclusively through ego or self-interest, whereas a generous thought looks at the situation through the lens of friendliness, wisdom and justice. A character can change radically when the self refers to the light of the soul.

To witness one's anger is an opportunity to realise one's wrong expectation from a situation. The energy saved may lead to courage, patience and wisdom − essential steps along the path of enlightenment.

Some of our subconscious experiences find their way into normal consciousness. A mature person experiences numerous minds or mental zones that co-exist. There are cases where, within the same person, two (or more) distinct personalities exist together. During episodes of stress or pain, different personalities emerge and cause considerable confusion — clinically referred to as 'dissociative identity disorder'. It demonstrates multi-mind views superimposed on each other. When the rational mind is in full use and the intellect is active then spiritual intelligence is likely to supersede other levels of the mind.

The dualism of body-mind or self-soul calls for human effort to interconnect them in the future and establish the harmony latent within the person.

As the self is disciplined and groomed through modesty, courage, accountability and reflection, thoughts begin to connect with higher consciousness through the heart. This enables the self to read and respond to situations more accurately and effectively. When emotional responses and inappropriate reactions are reduced and corrected, wise thoughts and actions will emerge.

Fears, uncertainties and insecurities emanate from the lower self and ego and are obstacles in the path of spiritual evolvement.

During most of one's lifetime, the ego/self is the leading principle. It is the source and the object of striving. It is also the cause of all emotions, feelings, sentiment and evaluations of good/bad and success/failure. Our identification with the ego/self (especially the body) is due to years of familiarity and attachment to this 'me'. Letting go of this shifting identity is therefore unimaginable, but displacing it with the higher self is possible and necessary for progress.

Power struggles and competition are due to separate identity and individuality which are in turn due to evolutionary distance from the primal force of life and unifying oneness.

Most religious and spiritual exercises emphasise the importance of a purified heart. In preparation for this the self must grow beyond negative emotions such as fear, greed, hatred, anger, enmity, insecurity, blame or guilt. These states will tarnish the heart and veil its potential luminance. The darkness of the self's night will disappear with the appearance of the dawn light of self-knowledge. The relationship between mind and heart is the most crucial issue in the spiritual evolvement of a human being.

To witness perfection we need synchrony between soul and self, through mind and heart.

The nature/nurture relationship is part of existential plurality and complementarity. Nature's hidden blueprint needs nurture for its pattern to emerge and evolve to its ultimate potential. Nature needs nurture to bring about the completion of the evolvement of the self to its soul. Both aspects relate and rely upon each other. Harmony between nature and nurture is optimum when the self's consciousness is brought into alignment with soul consciousness. Then sight and insight, head and heart, are in synchrony and harmony.

When the self is oriented towards the soul one can accept criticism and blame and is least concerned about reputation or image. Otherwise, self importance dominates and conditions the mind and one's conduct.

Higher consciousness beams at the self through the heart to stimulate it towards appropriate interpretation and action that lead towards spiritual awakening. The evolved self has harnessed lower impulses and the powers of attraction and repulsion. The power of attraction can lead to indulgence or other vices, such as obsessive asceticism, immoderation, instability, rigidity of mind, indifference or extravagance. When this power is controlled it becomes modesty, tranquillity and self-control.

Be aware of what you say and let your mind and heart be unified behind your speech.

The power of repulsion can manifest as anger, foolishness, overconfidence and arrogance. Other vices include cowardice, despair and inordinate submissiveness. When this power is harnessed, it brings out the virtues of courage, magnanimity, endurance and self-control.

The clearer the outer boundaries imposed upon the self, the greater the chance to experience inner boundlessness.

When courage and modesty are practised in personal conduct, then wisdom emerges and harnesses the vices of impudence, cunning, stupidity, dullness and sluggishness. With wisdom comes intelligence, retention, rationality and a greater capacity to learn and apply knowledge appropriately.

Every action and intention will leave its mark upon the mind and the self. Acting upon the lower tendencies darkens the heart, whereas virtuous action will purify the heart. The path of selfless service is universally acclaimed by spiritual seekers.

Like all other complementary dualities, a person's rights are inseparable from responsibilities. The same equation applies to societies and nations. The ultimate desire is to be healthy, content and a useful member of humanity. The first step towards this goal is to apply limitations upon the self through boundaries of conduct at all levels of body, mind and behaviour. By imposing limitations upon the self, the boundless domain of higher consciousness will open up to it. The hazier one's personal, ethical and moral grounds, the less likely the union of the self-soul.

A disciplined and evolved person lives according to personal boundaries and restrictions yet experiences inner openings to boundless domains.

A virtue or vice is meaningful in the context of a specific event or situation. The virtue of generosity becomes a vice if not tempered by discernment. An act of courage becomes foolhardiness if not guided by modesty, wisdom and justice. Virtue and vice are like the sloping road: which way is up or down depends on the way you are facing.

The self resents criticism for it loves the image of perfection. In truth the self is the image of the perfect soul, but how can a shadow ever be perfect?

Embarrassment, shame and guilt occur when our intention and action have deviated from a better course through awareness or hindsight. The discrepancy between what the self does and what the heart knows gives rise to the awareness called shame, regret or guilt. This guilt though resented, is a gift to the self to increase its awareness before action and bring into better alignment the head and heart through caution and reflection before emotional or irrational action.

Self correction requires a reliable and appropriate reference point and standard readily available, that is, the soul within the heart.

Human addictions cause much misery and disgrace to the person, as well as to society. Decadent lifestyles involving alcohol, irresponsible sex, gambling, obsessive and extreme sport and other abnormal behaviours and vices are rampant in modern societies due to the lack of a clear ethical map and moral direction. The root of all addiction is the innate passionate need of the self to unite with its soul-mate and be content. When not evolving in this direction, the self is distracted into false and futile obsessions. Outer worldly addictions give only temporary and false contentment whilst driving the self into deeper despair. All outer addictions are reinforced by habits and mental associations with pleasure and ease, which invariably lead to greater dis-ease. Enlightenment is the result of fulfilling the addiction of self to soul.

Abstention is hopeful in spiritual growth only when the self deliberately turns away from a desire or distraction which it can access and enjoy towards a higher cause (such as serving others).

Unexpected or strange human behaviour and complex emotions can be understood by referring to the self and soul model. At one end is the material, causal and worldly; at the other end is the spiritual, intangible and timeless. Each of these domains make their powerful demands upon a person. The self naturally responds to a hierarchy of needs as the self evolves towards its destiny. Appropriate reading and action in a situation occurs when the self refers to higher consciousness and follows the signs of the heart after passing through the reasons of the intellect.

When the ego has surrendered and consciousness expands beyond personal identity, then soul awareness is close at hand.

When the self is out of control like a wild horse, the skilled trainer will allow it to roam about for a while, then rein it in. Rebellion and obstinacy are natural to the childish self. Growth and evolvement of the self are the result of the constant discipline and reference to the higher self, reason, intellect and heart. Whenever a thought occurs it is modified and entrapped as mental energy. Thus, the task of the evolved being is to overcome this boxed in mental activity or ego that gives the self the illusion of developed identity and personality. Much of human behaviour is a function of the chemistry within the brain. With radical change in one's conduct there is also an effect upon brain chemistry. By physically smiling, for example, one can induce a feeling of wellbeing.

Residing within every person are numerous selves which are the cause of inner conflict, spilling out as inconsistent behaviour and confusion.

A strong personality often implies a dominant ego. Occasionally it could be due to a self that has surrendered to the soul. Ordinary people consider self doubt as a weakness, whereas for the seeker it is the first step that leads to inner certainty and unison. The average human being exerts a lot of effort in caring for the physical body, the mind, senses and other faculties. A clear and rational mind is a great asset with regards to worldly matters, but unless it is transcended it can slow down spiritual progress. It is said that paradise is full of simple people. Worldly wisdom requires a clear mind and an alert intellect. Heavenly wisdom needs a pure heart and trust in the perfection of the moment. Worldly maps and highway codes are mostly quantitative, whereas heavenly insights are mostly qualitative. A healthy and balanced person reads and follows both maps. Quality and quantity are ever-connected in the atlas of life.

A wise person draws strength from reflecting upon past mistakes, whereas the fool wishes to forget failures and is carried away by the occasional success.

When we talk about a character or personality, we generally imply the prevailing qualities in that person's behaviour. Cynicism is an easy, slippery route followed by the clever self to preserve itself and to avoid a challenging situation that may lead to selflessness (loss of self) and loss of ego. An angry, cowardly or indulgent person is one who has not harnessed the lower tendencies of the self. No character or behaviour is permanent, for when personal behaviour is altered, the character also changes. Spiritual practices can radically change old habitual actions or tendencies of a person. This happens more effectively with the help of a teacher or guide. Old undesirable traits and vices can change to virtuous actions with serious discipline and commitment to a new direction.

A hypocritical self cannot focus and witness the light of the soul within for it is distracted and absorbed by its ego image. You are either at the altar of your ego or in the soul's sanctum.

Responsible behaviour and selfless service are usually reliable conditions for reducing the grip of the lower self and increasing awareness and spiritual progress. The behaviour of a human being does reflect to a great extent the physical and emotional state of the person. We are much affected by our relationship to food and possessions, as well as our interest in higher values and the search for meaning. Outer abstentions and restrictions increase the potential for inner expansion. We often miss an inner opportunity due to the ego's constant desire for outer increase and expansion, as it tries to mimic the soul. An extrovert personality explores new horizons of experiences and increases in consciousness, whilst an introvert fears exposure and challenges to mind and self and therefore arrests the rise of consciousness. In reality, a person is a complex mosaic of traits and can never be identified solely as an introvert or extrovert.

A clear mind is a prelude to a pure heart. Selfless acts help to purify the heart and are preludes to better self and soul unison.

Personal identity and the constant reference to oneself as 'I' in ever-changing situations and circumstances are reinforced by personal consciousness identifying with a physical body, mind and memory. Reference to previous actions, thoughts and feelings produce this ego/self identification, whose core is based on memory, images and values. That is why we like to be reminded by photos of special events or roles which reinforce identity. A memory is likely to fade away unless it is reproduced in some way. Mental recall and its quality reflect one's inner state of mental hygiene and well-being.

Our idea of the self is a constructed myth. It is an image in the mind of the beholder and beholden. This is why we can say, 'I am beside myself today' or 'I never really knew him'.

When the self acknowledges humility, the soul will shine with its nobility. The self needs to be flexible, humble and submissive in order to resonate with the soul. A broken or fragmented psyche is not conducive for spiritual development. The human self contains the body, mind, intellect, heart and all other facets of mineral, plant and animal life. It also receives the soul's transmission with all its sublime patterns, meanings and perfect qualities. The wise person cares for the harmony and stability of the self and its relationship with the environment to give it ease and willingness to follow the 'voice within the heart'.

Sadness can lead to depression, happiness to mania, fear to phobia and concerns to paranoia. Darkness leads to gloom and light leads to hope.

The self can take on the negative attributes of meanness, arrogance and other egotistic traits when it faces the black hole of self assertion. The self will only cease to mimic and be a parody of the soul when it realises it is totally dependent upon it and gives up its own pretensions for acknowledgement and honour. Self-knowledge through supremacy of the soul will bring about durable contentment, which is the state of a healthy person witnessing the perfection of every moment in life.

The self can only be honoured when it identifies least with the body and mind and focuses on its perfect soul. The material side belongs to earth and the soul belongs to heaven.

The word 'person' is from the Greek *persona*, meaning 'mask'. The professional mask – with all its skills, training and social identification – plays a big role in creating self esteem and a stronger illusion of 'identity'. In that role the person attempts to present and preserve that 'persona'. Self awareness and identity occur in relationship with a role, an event, a value or a situation. The hierarchy of importance of the role or personal image relates to the absolute or ultimate reference within us – the soul. Veils of personality and multitudes of 'mindsets' are great obstacles and barriers to spiritual progress and salvation.

Personal consciousness is conditioned and changes constantly. It gains sustainable stability only by referring to soul consciousness.

Human beings desire to belong, to be loved, have a family and be part of a culture, organisation or nation. These expansive desires of the self are reflections of patterns contained within the soul to which we belong. A self is as good as its ability to take on the colours and qualities of the soul, by subduing the false egotistical appetite and its distractions from the purpose of life. When the self has fully divorced the ego and marries the soul, then it is higher than the angels. Otherwise, it sinks lower than the animals in its despairing darkness, aggression and violence.

Spiritual immaturity is the basic underlying factor in human discord, anger, intolerance and brutality. This outcome is the negative side of what nature intended.

The self needs to be occupied and desires to be acknowledged, for it is like a shadow without independence or durability. The incidence of depression or suicidal tendencies decrease during times of social struggle, strife and war because the self is occupied with survival and other urgent needs. There is a big difference between sublime reflectiveness and random idleness. Tourism and travel are means, for example, for the self to escape familiar habits and widen its horizons. Also, these activities can become in themselves habitual distractions from the life's task of the self to discover the soul and its boundless horizons. That happy conclusion can be speeded up if the self is restricted and controlled.

What is superficially labelled as an identity or personality or independence is due to a lack of unison between the self and soul. In truth one is totally dependent (self) and the other independent (soul).

The evolved self has the benefits of clear witnessing and monitoring situations in the outer world and within. A wise self refers frequently to reason, rationality and the heart. When you are angry the witnessing faculty of the heart takes a snapshot of the situation, whilst the inner monitor exercises a restraining influence. The heart then decrees the next step: to act or not, how and when. These developments accelerate according to one's spiritual growth, stability and cautious awareness of the pitfalls of the ego and its tricks. The rational mind awakens the faculty of the inner witnesser. The stable, 'authentic' person is guided by the unity of consciousness.

The self expands in moments of ease and pleasure– hence the expansion of breath in laughter. With anguish and pain the self contracts – hence the restriction of breath in crying.

The self fears death due to its identification with the growing body. Although we do not fully understand the nature of death, we practise mini-deaths with every sleep or deep meditation. Eternal life is experienced beyond the threshold of death, in the zone of the ongoingness of the hereafter. The way to paradise or hell referred to in religions often relate to the state of contentment or confusion of the heart at the point of death. A pure heart implies awakened god consciousness and union between self and soul. A dark and fearful heart implies confusion of the self and the absence of inner light, which is akin to the state of hell.

Aggression relates to despondency and occurs when the self is deprived of the soul's life force. Kindness and love is the reverse, when the self overflows with the soul's generosity.

The sincere seeker prefers solitude to socialising, abstinence to indulgence, modesty to greed. He is self-effacing, humble, balanced, mild in manner, compassionate and selfless. The evolved seeker is least concerned with self-image, frivolous worldly pleasures, luxuries and egotistic desires. Thus, absence from oneself is the door to realising the soul's ever-present and divine grace. Then one is at the threshold of the authentic self, basking in the light of supreme consciousness.

Every role the self plays is a mistaken identity, for it changes. What is permanent and true is the soul, which is the greatest divine gift and grace bestowed upon humanity.

3.3. JOURNEY OF THE SELF

A baby drops into the world and experiences consciousness at numerous levels and ways. An old person drifts out of this world towards another domain of consciousness, only vaguely resembling our physical world.

Every human journey is a unique path between earthly defined boundaries leading to the subtle realm of energy and angels. Most people, however, dash from life to death with years wasted in between. Every entity in creation is on a journey with a specific beginning and an end in time. The human journey begins with the physiological, biological, chemical and other processes and developments. The intellect grows with emotional maturity and from experiencing interactions in the world of cause and effect. With wisdom, insight and higher consciousness, spirituality becomes a way of life.

The process of biological evolution is as old as life on earth. Spiritual evolution could only begin with the rise of self consciousness and the inner desire to unite personal and pure consciousness.

Human nature straddles two levels of consciousness: one is eternal timelessness and encompasses the universe, the other is specific and conditioned to the changing world of time and space. The self relies on personal consciousness, whilst higher consciousness is ever present within the heart. Spiritual evolvement occurs within the sacred space of the heart where worldly gravity unites with heavenly levity and soul consciousness.

The main challenge in life is to bring into harmony chemistry of the head with the lights within the heart. When the self is aligned with the soul, this triumphant union reveals itself as enlightenment.

In truth every instant is perfect but we judge a situation through the self's expectations, misconceptions and ignorance. When there are desires and needs to be fulfilled, the self views delays and obstacles as misfortunes to be overcome, rather than opportunities to respond to appropriately and adjust intentions and direction. Delays are not denials. But at the physical level the body is impatient for well beingness and the mind for ease.

Isolation, dislocation, abstention, reduced social connections and outer action can all help in spiritual evolvement and growth.

The human journey begins with a limited and restricted world where the priority is physical survival and growth of the body and the childish ego personality. The evolution of self and mind starts by discriminating differences in the outer world, then differentiating between entities and events and their causal relationships. The growth is only completed by discovering the unifying essence of all.

Grappling with dualities implies less vision of unity.

A child's preoccupation is almost entirely with food, comfort and pleasurable interaction with the immediate surroundings. The foetus in the womb is in natural submission to its conducive environment. The nascent self is totally dependent on its genetic, biological, neurological and hormonal programmes and is in a state of submission, relaxed and confident. At this level we witness harmony and unity due to surrender and acceptance.

Innocent children are endearing, as the self has not yet developed into a stubborn, selfish ego. Innocence is ignorance due to inexperience – forgivable and charming.

When the child is born he or she is outwardly dependent,

primarily on the mother. Horizons of outer dependencies widen within a few years with the realisation of the need for food, love, clothes, shelter and other physical requirements for comfort, as well as emotional and social needs. The mother's early concern is to arouse a response in the baby by soliciting a reaction through sound, movement, intimate hugs and other connecting gestures and acts. Life manifests as responding to change.

Childish meanness and cruelty are due to the self's lack of evolvement and self awareness. Early years are ruled by the ego and conditioned consciousness.

With age memory loss increases, except for certain childhood episodes, games played, gifts received or special holidays and treats enjoyed. Nature has programmed the human journey for the mind to go beyond memory and the recollection of events. The deepest memory is to go to its roots and origins: the primal pure consciousness before it was personalised and diverted into senses and mind.

The human being journeys along a spectrum of consciousness, which include physical, psychological, emotional, intellectual and spiritual levels.

The body is composed of numerous physical and chemical materials, ranging from simple molecules to complex structures. The vegetative domain includes the usual plant functions of absorbing nutrients, expelling toxins, growth, reproduction and decomposition. The animal functions include mobility, will, emotions and higher consciousness. Human beings contain the designs, programmes and consciousnesses of all discernable creations in this world. No entity outside of the self can be comprehended, unless its essence or pattern is already engrained within the soul. Thus, in truth, whatever one discovers in the outer world is due to its 'blueprint' replica being present within the soul. The ultimate maturity in consciousness is when the two states of outer and inner meet in a new light of unity.

With discipline and guidance, the self begins to take on aspects of the quality of the soul. With total surrender to the soul, the self will reflect the soul's great attributes.

As the child's reasoning faculties develop, so will its knowledge of interdependence and response to the various stimuli that lead to desirable or undesirable outcomes. The powers of attraction and repulsion and the desire for certain results or outcomes dominate. By the time one is around forty years of age the experience of interdependence and the knowledge of how to manoeuvre in this world (in form and meaning) are usually well practised and developed. A successful, healthy person will know how to encourage, lead (or mislead) using past memories, experience and reasoning, as is relevant to the specific environment, society and culture.

With maturity and wisdom the power of the ego is weakened and the self rendered more receptive to referring to the heart and soul consciousness.

Emotional maturity comes with physical growth and the development of rationality and wisdom. The shell of a plant needs to break open to enable the kernel to grow and yield its future flowers and fruits. The self too need to discard its egotistic shell and be watered and fed by the light of higher consciousness. To spiritually 'educate' is to 'draw out' what is already in the soul. We need to draw upon and refer to that which is in us and rely upon it in our life's progress. Body, mind, senses, memory, intentions and actions are the means by which the self navigates along the outer world towards the safe harbour of the inner heart. The self evolves through the macro world of the rational mind to the infinitely small microcosm of the inner soul.

If the self does not turn away from its egotistic lower tendencies towards the higher soul, it is not fulfilling its purpose in life.

The innocence of a child is due to its natural ignorance. The apparent innocence of an enlightened being is due to his focus upon the perfection within a situation, hence lacking the fear of outcome, reputation or other self concerns and interest. The focus of the enlightened being is upon the soul and its ever-present perfections without ignoring the specific and limited levels of consciousness.

Altruism is a unique human behaviour, where the evolved self serves others and sacrifices itself. The enlightened person's self is submerged within the soul and as such is beyond selfishness or selflessness.

To celebrate the birthday of a child is to pander to the ego, which is necessary for the childish self to grow. However, for the grown up person the ego is a matter of shame. For the wise person, what is there to celebrate other than awakening to witnessing perfection in creation. Whoever has attained that state does not care for birth or death; the eternal light of the soul overrides all these worldly moving shadows.

It is personal and conditioned consciousness that produces one's personality.

Every human being has a personality but with spiritual awakening one's flexibility and compassion increases and the higher self begins to dominate the baser one. The enlightened human being sees things as they are without personal or emotional values interfering with the facts and realities. The heart is used as a navigational console, whilst the soul is the power house and direction finder leading to the shore of contentment.

To drive cheerfully along the highways of knowledge and perfection you must leave behind the polluted district of the lower self.

Ambition is a major life force which ceases with death. Its direction changes with self evolvement, knowledge, experience and wisdom. No amount of outer success and security will remove entirely the occasional feelings of confusion, gloom or despondency. Inner access to heart and soul is beyond worldly success or failure. It is a state of joyful contentment that is not dependent upon the world of change and uncertainty.

Our senses explore sights, sounds, touch, smell and taste, as windows connecting the outer world to the mind and heart.

For the self to relate to and understand the outer world correctly it needs to exercise modesty, friendship, mildness, patience, self-discipline and love of truth. Courage is the foundation of magnanimity, endurance and self-reliance. Wisdom is the result of modesty and courage, which engenders rationality and clarity in understanding. Justice is the crown and the source of wisdom, growth, awareness, insights, subtle learning and amicability.

The quality of your evaluation and response to the outer world mirrors your inner state.

The self becomes more reliant upon the rational mind and heart with spiritual maturity and wisdom. It also looks to the heart and soul for higher knowledge and trust. The baby or child has no fear of death and even talks about it matter of factly and unemotionally. Later on, as an adult he dreads this unknown but inevitable event. The wise and illumined person is neutral regarding death and is positive about life's ongoingness hereafter.

The most important and wise preparation in this life is cheerful readiness to leave this world at the appointed time. Death is simply a transformation to another state, whose seeds are sown at birth and come to fruit at the end of one's life.

The human self is like a complex city encompassing the sky above as well as the ocean below. The arteries and other organs are the energy conveyors and converters, whereas the nervous system is the communications network, culminating in the outer and inner senses. The soul is the heavenly king, which resides in the heart. Its government is headed by the self and its functionaries perform their duties with the objective of preserving the safety and unity of the domain whilst developing and evolving the kingdom. The self is at best the earthly loyal agent of the heavenly soul, which is its source of nourishment and growth. When the self is in full submission to its master, the kingdom is secure and peaceful.

The self loves to explore and discover the root of all things, always restlessly yearning for its own origin – the soul at heart.

The natural human tendency to look for miracles and the supernatural is simply a reflection of the vast domain of the unseen, with its amazing ways which are beyond human reasoning and understanding. Confusion occurs when the worldly and heavenly maps and codes are mixed up, resulting in 'mysticism', obscurantism or superstition. The world will reveal itself according to the level of perception and consciousness of the recipients; as does the heavenly unseen world.

Evolution is the transformation of a transient earthly entity towards regaining its original heavenly identity according to its soul's level of consciousness.

The linear, earthly, gravitational world follows certain

predictable natural laws within space-time. This macro world is subject to the laws of general relativity. The subatomic micro world can only be understood through the laws of quantum physics, probabilities, uncertainties and other peculiarities, which are most incongruous as far as our natural macro world is concerned. Each domain has its rules, and their meeting point is within the unified human consciousness. Personal consciousness relates to the natural gravitational world. The subtler, pure or soul consciousness relates to the unseen world of particle physics and the other intangible fundamentals of creations.

The human heart is where the earthly and heavenly domains meet and unite, peacefully.

One Sufi model of the journey of the self describes four phases. The first is from dualities towards the subtler dimension of unified meanings. The self leaves behind emotions, values, expectations and moves from the physical to the mental and on to spiritual lights. This journey leaves the confusion of multiplicity, choices and actions and reaches the abode of unity.

The self is never content, unless it is on the path of pursuing meanings through selfless acts and services, beyond its direct needs and worldly interests.

The second stage of the journey is to be in the divine presence exclusively and to witness all the perfect qualities and attributes. The self sees the world now through the lens of the perfect one seer, hears through the one hearer and knows through the all knowing. In this state the ego has vanished and intoxication with the truth envelops the being. This is the bewildering state of thrills and joys, which are beyond worldly understanding or reason. It is spiritual 'madness'.

The search for a better life is a reflection of the self's search for perfect alignment with the soul, where the outer and inner are in total harmony and unison.

The third stage of the journey is from the creator to creation and denotes the traveller's understanding and knowledge of the universe and its microcosmic holographic representation: the human soul. The world of change and complementary opposites is encompassed by divine mercy, generosity and constancy. The whole cosmos is held by, and oscillates around, energy beams characterised by god's great attributes and qualities ingrained within the human soul.

Where and how you are along your journey describes who you are.

The final or fourth stage is the station of the great prophets, messengers and enlightened masters. It is to return to be amongst creation as a servant and representative agent or steward of the creator. Service to humanity is based on submission and reference to the master of creation. Truth is now seen in all situations. This is the state of unity with the source and essence, which permeates all of existence. It is the state of annihilation in the one and ongoing by the one. The self is absorbed by the soul, then personal identity is lost in divine unity. This is the state of true authenticity and the human being is acting as god's shadow on earth.

An enlightened teacher is pleased with the good conduct or behaviour of a student for the student's sake – he already knows the perfect qualities inherent in the soul and as such cannot be truly impressed with mere progress towards this ever present truth.

Religion can be a hindrance to spiritual growth, unless taken seriously and applied sincerely and honestly. Otherwise, it is like sitting in a toy car that does not transport you to your destination. A fulfilled person drifts wisely out of the world of duality into the world of insight in readiness for departure into the hereafter. The wise and prepared person regards death as a doorway to the gardens of the heavenly abode.

The journey of the seeker is marked by numerous spiritual stepping stones, but arrival is marked by the end of all departures.

Life's purpose is to celebrate the glorious eternal one creator, whose qualities and attributes are the meaning and purpose of existence and whose supreme consciousness is the cause of all creation. The ultimate goal is for the human self to be in unison with the soul, which is but a small reflection of the perfect creator; like the one ocean drop that carries the qualities of the ocean. After the death of the body, the soul and its companion self return to the heavenly pool from where they had emerged in the first place, to witness subtler perfections.

Death is the transformation of the self from the space-time nursery to the domain of permanence and the life of eternal lights.

4. RELATIONSHIPS

It is due to relationships between creation, people, actions and knowledge that the human self evolves and cultures and societies grow and decay.

Everything in creation is interconnected by subtle and discernable links. All creations relate and interact with changing degrees of influence within space-time. These interactive relationships occur within each individual entity or system and between different species or clusters, groups and wider varieties of creations. They affect the quality and quantity of matter and energy fields internally and externally in the environment. Chemical, physical, electrical and other subtler links are the connecting mediums for these interactions. Everything pulsates, oscillates and resonates at different levels within the universe but the degree and extent of activation of these connections changes and varies in both simple and complex ways in relation to spatial extent and time.

The process of interaction between human beings is like mirrors in the making, where each mirror exerts some influence over the outcome of interactions. A farmer tries to provide the appropriate environment for his plant; a mother wishes a stable and safe place for the new born; a teacher tries to stimulate, discipline and train young minds. Every entity appears, evolves, grows, interacts and then dies, and these cycles repeat continuously.

A family, society or nation is more than the sum of its members. The societal mind or collective consciousness has a persistent durability and is different to the individual mind's flexibility and willingness to change. Profound forces preserve traditions, cultures and old ways within every social structure, with some allowance for absorbing new influences and trends, in form as well as meaning. What matters most in every situation are the higher durable values of wisdom, justice, love of truth and the spiritual health of individuals and society. Durable relationships are based on honesty, openness, accountability, ethical conduct and a higher purpose in life that binds people together in harmony and hope.

The root of every aspect of love, affection, connection or understanding is a reflection of an aspect of the original oneness or sameness in essence and unity at source.

4.1. CONNECTIVITY

What the self perceives has its original blueprint within the soul, which is being activated by experience and relationships in the outer world.

Every idea, intention, thought or behaviour is based on natural connections between what is experienced and the experiencer. It is through the activation of connections between intention and action that a specific experience occurs. Everything within the cosmic web is connected but which channel is being activated and for how long is what determines the outcome of the event and personal experience.

A situation occurs when channels of energies and physical movements are activated. This is also the situation with memory and emotions. The foundation for everything is already there but what appears is only due to movement of energy in those channels.

The universe and all that exists within it are described by relationships and the power of interaction between them. Whatever exists relates to something else and is never isolated, even though it has a specific identity, autonomy or apparent independence. Wholeness in life depends upon the harmonious dynamics of interdependence at all times. The only absolute independent and self-sustaining entity is god, who creates, contains and controls all of creation without being conditioned or affected. The divine supreme consciousness permeates all creations and is their essence.

God is the absolute unique eternal light illuminating all that there is in the universe. Truth is a beam of that divine light that beckons to itself.

The appearance of specific entities, forms or substances occur within the realm of space-time; they have a specific duration with a beginning and an end, during which period energy and matter interchange takes place on numerous levels. Every definable entity, form or person is subject to the flow of time, marked by birth, movement, maturity and death. All relationships and entities are constantly changing and have no durable 'constancy', 'static' security or reliability. Everything in motion is relative and all creation is subject to movement, which eventually returns to stillness.

All experiences and relationships lead towards inner and outer convergence and unison or divergence and dispersion.

The natural laws of attraction, repulsion and gravity are measurable aspects of the physical relationships between objects. In particle physics there are numerous relationships based on a multitude of fields, energy and minute impulses, such as an electron's direction of spin. The electromagnetic field governs the relationship between charged particles. Other dynamics in the galaxies and heavenly constellations are beyond perception or measurement. The situation reaches a point beyond human logic or ability to understand when movements approach the speed of light, or when mass touches infinity. Also, with changes in temperature and pressure, particles and molecules behave rather differently. At absolute zero temperature different atoms behave as though they are similar entities. It is as though when we are at the physical boundaries of the material world identities get lost and the unifying essence overwhelms differentiations.

There are different sets of laws for different levels of existence. What is natural in our day-to-day world does not apply in the subatomic world or in astrophysics.

In quantum mechanics and in certain other circumstances connections occur beyond spatial separation, giving rise to ideas regarding a unified theory in physics. Besides the worldly 'gravitational', 'relativistic' characteristics and 'quantum mechanics' foundations, the human being is subject to the 'uncertainty principle' in both the inner and outer dimensions. As human beings we are constantly driven towards unity and gatheredness. At birth there was no experience of self awareness (duality), or causality, but with maturity we experience separation and duality in life, whilst yet seeking unity and connectivity.

Unity can only be discerned through separation. All apparent outer disconnections are in fact subtly connected.

Our love for harmony, peace and perfection are all different manifestations of the power of love that drives us all to climb the ladder of life towards the pinnacle of the unifying essence. The bottom of this ladder rests upon the earth of the lower self or ego. The higher rungs are above the rational self and meet the soul in its heavenly abode. Everyone seeks connections in high places. We need to discover that the soul is the highest and most perfect heavenly entity which dwells within us. The desire to be in the company of the wealthy, famous and powerful is a reflection of the state of the soul that contains the patterns of boundless power and wealth. Equally, most religious minded people like to think their prayers are answered, so as to increase their faith or trust in god.

Rationality and logic, as practiced daily, are only an earthly reflection of divine supra-logic beyond the humanly conceived version.

All aspects of love relate to connectedness and knowledge of the one source. Through the soul, the power of love energises every human being and transmits all the primal patterns and designs of existence. The partnership of self and soul is a symbiotic one and is similar to that between light and shadow. The self/ego assumes its independence, although it owes life to its soul. The supreme consciousness connects heaven and earth, absolute and relative, seen and unseen, beyond time and within space-time. The self desires experiences which are 'breathtaking' or 'unbelievable', as attempts to transcend its limited consciousness. The earthly self evolves towards the heavenly soul. The self's conditioned consciousness always seeks boundless higher consciousness.

Love relates to knowledge and high consciousness while hate is based upon ignorance and disconnectedness.

The self loves to give and to receive. The quality or energy field of generosity is already there in the space around us but there is a need to bring about the connection between this energy frequency and personal consciousness. Generosity is needed for the self to awaken to wider horizons. The numerous qualities sought by the self are already there but one needs to 'tune' in to that specific spectrum or 'bandwidth' of attribute to attain the appropriate resonance and harmony.

God's attributes are the energy channels and beams which bring about discernment and knowledge to the sentient world.

Ten years ago I referred to myself as 'I', yet even after much change and growth, I still refer to myself as 'I'! When angry, you call yourself 'I', when content and at peace you still call yourself 'I'! The implication is that there is a core within you that is constant. This centre is the soul's consciousness. Growth and evolvement relate to changes in the body, the senses, mind, heart and intellect, discerned through conditioned consciousness or self. The ever restless self seeks its abode of security and rest with the soul at heart. Mental confusion and outer disturbances can be natural triggers or propellants for the self to seek inner peace and harmony. The move from head to heart is like turning from chaos to order.

The oldest memory is before the occurrence of the first memory. This foundation lies within soul consciousness, which is primal and not subject to time.

Consciousness and awareness widen and deepen with time, far beyond the material limitation of form and physical boundaries. Our mental health relates to the quality of our thoughts and emotions. Our social skills and maturity are assessed by our enjoyment and ease in relationships with other people. Social needs, acknowledgement and integration are aspects of belonging. In truth the self belongs to its soul. Emotional stability relates to the evolvement of the rational mind, beyond emotions and mood changes. Spiritual maturity relates to one's stead-fastness in the face of major outer changes, disturbances, failures and other difficulties. A spiritually evolved person feels normal emotions but does not succumb to emotional neurosis or break-downs. Pain is regarded as a natural warning, rather than a cause of suffering.

Whatever is perceived or experienced outwardly has its original root within the soul and is activated by the stimulus of a relationship between the outer and inner worlds.

In order to understand others we need to know ourselves better because the same pattern applies to all human beings. In form, shape and culture, everyone is different yet we are the same in our quest for health, contentment and happiness. Each human being has the potential to understand other beings because of the similarity of our souls, which carry god's perfect qualities. Thus, to know yourself means to know your soul and thereby the creator of your soul.

Most human beings admire a person in pursuit of higher fulfilment. Our natural tendency is to help the seeker of truth, rather than the seeker of outer wealth.

Good companionship, friendship or partnership draw the self closer to emotional and rational equilibrium, as well as to inner stability. Conflict, anger and blame are missed opportunities to understand a situation clearly. Accusing people for causing suffering is shifting the blame from ignorance of a situation and inappropriate action and thereby reinforcing the ego and its darkness. Honest accountability, self-reflection and personal responsibility teach us a great deal regarding the relationship between intentions, actions and the resultant outcomes. A person's outer relationships are as good as the alignment and relationship between the self and soul. Unless you realise the divine nature of the soul, other people's lives will not be revered or held sacred.

Interaction with others is necessary for the learning process of inner and outer equilibrium.

Thus, to know your soul and therefore your lord, you need to work through all the shadows and images of the self or ego. Indeed, the light which energises these shadows is the soul itself. To fulfil a need or a desire is one step towards harmony and contentment, but when will the self ever be desireless? Contentment is not in the nature of the self, unless it surrenders to the soul. Access to the soul is through a purified heart; for that reason most religious and spiritual practices aspire to bring about a wholesome heart. A purified heart enables the soul to beam at the self, body, mind, senses and intellect. This enables the person to have the best opportunity to be in harmony inwardly and outwardly.

The heart's light increases when the self is less concerned with outer worldly concerns, desires, and other distractions.

When the self is in unison with the soul one sees other people having similar needs and the same potential. Caring for others then becomes like caring for one's higher self by serving to uplift others. In truth there is no otherness, except in temporary outer appearances. There is one creator, one divine light, one lord, one universal soul from which countless souls have emerged, yielding the patterns of perfection and attributes of the one universal soul and supreme consciousness. The apparent outer dispersion is the shadow of eternal gatheredness.

Only by seeing other people as souls (i.e. the same as you) can you be generous, patient, clement and act with love and justice. Unless you see others as yourself, there is always potential conflict and discord.

In human relationships, one is sometimes content by depending upon others, while at other times one prefers self-reliance. Sometimes one welcomes the dependence of someone else upon oneself. At other times this dependence may be resented. What lies behind the vice of 'biting the hand that feeds you' is the truth that no person is ever the provider. God alone is the true source of all provisions; at best a person is a means of distributing, helping or serving others. These acts are akin to serving one's own higher self by reducing selfishness and egotistical indulgences. Indeed, love and care for others increases love of the self for its inner soul-mate.

Any action that leads towards greater reliance on god is a virtuous act.

Self-love is the primary motive behind all endeavours. The question is, which self is doing the self-loving? How can you love a greedy self? The self that deserves love is the higher self, or soul itself where all the desirable qualities and perfections are imprinted. Yet, love of the higher self is balanced and enhanced by repulsion from the lower self. Suffering from darkness may lead to light and virtue. The nature of the self is pathetic when alienated from the soul. Such an estrangement is the cause of most psychological disorders.

To negate the negative is the first step towards establishing the positive.

In all relationships we try to attract that which is desirable and to repel that which is not. What we like and dislike depends upon temporary needs and habits, real or artificial, which change according to time and place. In fact, what the self dislikes may turn out to be the best tonic for one's inner growth, while that which the self desires may be its poison. To act effectively in any situation you need to consider the overall context. For physical health you need to refer to a good doctor. When the heart is tarnished, one needs to regret, repent, reconcile and take counsel with someone who is spiritually wiser. Difficult situations may require an appropriate teacher or guide. It is a natural human tendency to follow a teacher or a role model. If this relationship is based upon mutual respect, trust and affection, then hearts and minds connect and resonate efficiently. Loyalty, honesty, patience and selflessness are needed for a successful outcome in transmitting wisdom.

Isolation can bring about desolation, dislocation and greater egocentricity. Yet, openings and insights can result from periods of disciplined confinement and timely isolation.

Difficult relationships, discordance or conflict, whether between individuals or societies, implies incompatible components, states and systems that do not connect or relate. Natural order is based on connectedness, harmony and appropriate links. Whatever we encounter in existence is maintained through connecting threads of the unifying field of life. The supreme consciousness energises creation, both at a hierarchical level, as well as hetrarchical. Although we often perceive divine power emanating from top to bottom, it is equally true that it occurs from bottom to top, as well as from the centre to the peripheries and vice versa. The cosmic consciousness is within all and everything is within it.

Stability and harmony implies an appropriate fit; rejection and discord is the result of a misfit.

Marriage is an attempt to increase the stability, harmony and wholesomeness of two separate beings who are seeking contentment and happiness in a world of constant change and uncertainty. Its success depends on the partners helping each other to tap the inner source of contentment and peace within their hearts. A partner is of great help if the relationship leads to effective alignment and unison between the self and its soul. Initially, marriage may be due to physical, cultural or other attractions, but its growth and maturity into a deep, and harmonious relationship depends on each partner's commitment to wholesomeness of body, mind and heart. Falling passionately in love with someone diverts the self temporarily from the innate love of the self for the soul within. The origin of all outer love is the primal love of self for its soul.

The human heart is the most unique creation. It can harbour gatheredness and contentment or be veiled by egotistic darkness.

It is remarkable how much attention and energy we give to outer worldly relationships, yet how feeble is our effort for the union and permanent marriage of the self with its soul. If this inner relationship is successful, then the wholesome and unified person can deal appropriately with all other relationships. If one is truly happy within oneself then one is likely to be cheerful with others.

If you are not 'one', how can you deal with 'anyone'?

Effective or transformative communication occurs when the connection between transmission and reception of the signals is at a deep level. Miscommunication happens when this connection is broken, or becomes faulty or distorted by interference. Asking her son if he loves her, a sick mother may actually simply desire reassurance that he will continue to support her. Often what our language and voice produce is only the surface of what the self is really concerned with. Social conditioning, fear and expectation cause much of the difficulties we experience in relationships and communication.

All relationships are mirrors reflecting inner states, although we often ignorantly blame or judge the outer world for being at fault without awareness of our inner confusion.

The outside world is experienced through the lens of the self/mind's interpretation of outer events and situations as transmitted through the senses. Mental processing uses past values, relying upon previous experiences in order to relate to present ones. A highly-charged electrical storm will interfere with radio reception and warning systems. The sky can become a dangerous place for a small aeroplane in a cyclone, as this causes disorientation, instrument errors and other malfunctions. Likewise there are faulty connectedness between the different human senses and outer world events. The mind and intellect need to be in optimum condition in order to respond appropriately to the signals and signs around us. Connections are universal but what matters most are the activated and energised links within this pulsating interactive outer and inner world. The door to optimum connectivity is for the self to be in tune with soul consciousness.

A contented heart is the door and threshold to the higher openings of intuition, inner sense and pure consciousness.

4.2. INTERACTIVE MIRRORS

There is no action without a reaction. You cannot sense or perceive anything outside of yourself unless it has generated an impression within you. Outer and inner states mirror and reflect each other constantly.

Every human self grows as a living, evolving image or shadow of the soul and as a mirror of the outer world, reflecting and responding to what is cast upon it. Each self is in continuous dynamic interaction with its body, mind, heart and soul, as well as with the outer world and prevailing environment. Transmissions and receptions occur all the time at numerous tangible and subtle levels. The quality of the mirror is dependant upon the alignment between its outer surface and the inner coating composed of heart and soul. The earthly images are reflected by the self and the heavenly ones are reflected by the soul. To function efficiently the self needs the light of the soul and its high consciousness. The state (purity) of the heart is a good indicator of the quality of the mirror's coating.

When outside images impact upon the surface self, like a mirror it reflects its response according to the quality of its inner coating (self-soul unison).

Earth, water, air and fire contain the four natural qualities of dry, wet, cold and hot, which correspond to the tangible states of the self. The self is in healthy equilibrium when these qualities balance and complement each other. The soul radiates its pure consciousness, which is conditioned and modified by the self as it energises body, mind and heart. The relationship between self and soul is like a royal marriage; their union signifies a stable kingdom.

Soul consciousness is connected directly to the perfect divine qualities; the self desires and pursues these qualities outwardly. The self is intrinsically programmed to unite with its soul.

The soul beams all the desirable qualities and attributes ascribed to god, such as compassion, mercy, generosity, forgiveness, ability and power. When the self is aligned with the soul it absorbs and reflects these qualities efficiently and harmoniously. When the self is inattentive to the soul, then it reflects the darkness of the ego and other shadowy images. The self, in its low state, reflects opposite attributes to those of the soul. The ego represents entrapped images and negative traits. The self wants to be seen with the qualities of the soul, even though it has turned away from it. It desires a reputation of generosity, rather than meanness. The self dislikes a person or situation that causes it to behave selfishly or egotistically. It loves the soul even though it may behave differently.

Look for the root of deviation, opposition and duality which gives the ego its energy and identity and you will begin to see perfection through the lens of unity.

The healthy development of the person's living mirror is key to one's ability to relate properly and effectively to the outer images cast upon it. It is our duty to keep this mirror strong (body), clean (mind) and polished (heart), so that it is always able to interact and reflect with efficiency and excellence. Unison of self and soul is the root foundation of quality reflections. If this is achieved, then other images will make sense as they nullify, relate or unify with mind and heart. The self needs stability, clarity and wholesomeness to reflect the truth appropriately. An image from a mirror can be conditioned, contaminated, modified, deflected, refracted and reflected. There is always some undue interference or interaction with other shadows and images in the vicinity. The self is a continual 'work in progress.' The soul is its altar.

A mind is like an organic garden: your work is to control the weeds and feed the seedlings with natural and sustainable means.

Outer images are mediated by the five outer senses, which are like rivers leading into the inland lake of combined senses, where they all meet and reach the mind to relate, evaluate and interpret outer experience and meaning. The mind, then, gives value and importance to the experience and files it in the short-term memory. With the growth and evolvement of the rational mind, the self becomes more aligned to the soul. Increased grooming in modesty, courage, wisdom and justice will help to open the inner heart, letting the light of higher consciousness shine upon the self stronger.

The light of the pure heart gives clarity and meaning to the facts and events experienced by the self.

Life's experiences and responses are much affected by the state of the heart. The same scenery evokes different feelings and reactions at different times and in different people. The open desert uplifts the heart of those who love endless space but can depress the farmer living on the edge of the encroaching sand dunes. All worldly experiences and events are challenges and reminders of the self to evolve and constantly refer to intellect, heart and soul. We are all programmed to want better. The soul is always best.

Through relationships with people, ideas, actions, knowledges and experiences the self evolves and matures.

When the self admits that its judgement of outer events and responses to them reflect its inner state, then awareness beyond the ego and self-image become spontaneous. Inner evolvement is speeded up by regular reflection and reference to the higher consciousness. We perceive new experiences in accordance with our updated mental values and state. No two images are the same because of the constant changes that take place in one's inner state, as well as in the outer situation. A quick opinion is a vain attempt to reduce what is naturally diverse (personal views) to a singular, fixed, personal view.

New experiences are related to what has already been evaluated and stored in the mind. As such, the mind is both a reliable reference point as well as an obstruction to new values.

Interactions and relationships in this world help to reveal the meaning and purpose of existence, struggles, transitions and the constant drive towards attaining durable ease, peace and joy. Every human experience contains a message, which is often ignored or superimposed upon by a judgement, due to our egotistical and lazy mindset. We often dismiss an unpleasant message or deny failures. The self wants a constant state of joy, which belongs to the soul and not to the world of learning and evolving. Shyness, shame, regret and guilt are signs of the self being aware of the inadequacy of its actual performance in comparison with the perfections within the soul.

At the present moment you are the outcome of past action, intention and thought. The future depends upon your present and renewed intention and vision.

Parents, teachers, spiritual and religious guides have a difficult task in assessing the extent to which they should allow a young person to deviate from the traditional moral and ethical norms. Monastic life is one extreme remedy to extinguish the desires and lust of the self. The other extreme is to allow the self to experience the whole range of distractions and decadent behaviour, in the hope of its outgrowing such deviations. The main danger is that the mind may become distorted and unhealthy habits may set in deeply. A strict, stoic regime will work if the self is happy with the lack of exposure to 'normal' life and has no secret regrets or desires. Most teachers advocate moderate exposure to lower tendencies and encourage their students to focus on higher virtues and develop a taste for them.

We possess some inner navigational aids and skills, such as intuition, insights, feelings and inner inspiration, that guide us to the safety of the heart.

The evolving self progresses towards its destiny when the heart is cleansed and the shadows of the ego rendered like distant mirages. Then, this reliable or illumined self is ruled by the soul, whose light shines upon it without the shadows of emotions, conflicts, confusion and other interfering images. This is the elixir of transformation that we all seek: the base metal of the self being transmuted into the golden soul.

There is a difference between looking into a mirror to ensure one's cleanliness or neatness and looking to admire one's self and its outer appearance.

It is natural for the self to long for contentment and tranquillity. Any personal need that is referred to the soul, god or higher consciousness is an authentic and legitimate need. Any desire that gives the self the illusion of its independence or freedom from the soul is an artificial and regrettable desire. When the self is subservient and humble to the soul, it is energised and is healthy. When it rebels and asserts its independence (falsely), then it is wayward, restless and confused.

The self is always insecure until it is fully aligned with the soul, which is ever-secure and content. This is inner harmony and peace.

When a disagreeable situation arises, the self tries to justify itself and blame others or bad luck. Being challenged by an unacceptable or changeable outer situation gives the self an opportunity to change its outlook or expectation. When the self faces the soul, it shines like a full moon reflecting the sun's light from all its surface. The self takes on the colours of the soul's qualities of courage, love, modesty, friendliness and generosity. When soul consciousness is absent, personal consciousness is dim. The dark moon is then deprived of the sun and in this state the self behaves as an ego with fear, hate, meanness, suspicion, anger and other dark traits.

A confused self is like a tarnished mirror, where new outer images do not register well. This 'sick' mirror needs restoration through realignment with heart and soul.

Appropriate relationships with creation come about from clear observation and rational evaluation of the situation and context. The root of most personal conflict is the notion of otherness, forgetting that all human beings have the same needs and potential. Differences are mostly outward and relate to body, mind and culture. Essentially we human beings are the same at heart or soul level. Whatever is witnessed outwardly has its patterns within us, for otherwise it could not be understood. What we hate in a person is often what we fear or hate in our own selves. All souls are in essence the same and human differences are due to the self and mind. When you see the sameness in people, understanding, love and compassion for all of creation follows. Our expectation of equality and justice is due to this innate knowledge of the sameness of all souls.

When you detest a specific behaviour in someone, see that vice in yourself first before you criticise or blame. This reflectiveness leads to wisdom and spiritual maturity.

When two people relate in a positive or complementary manner to one other, they act like two radios resonating together by emitting and receiving sounds which reinforce each other. Every human being both broadcasts waves, energies, auras, subtle signals and receive messages which either attract (good chemistry) or repulse (bad vibrations). It is natural for a family or society with a common culture, interests, needs and values to respond similarly in a situation. A mother can fully understand the grief of a woman who has lost her child. The human mirror responds (empathy) to a situation according to its own past images, values and memory. Conversely, when the self cannot relate to or understand images and messages flashed upon it, it becomes confused or even angry. Active listening to and empathy with others is a natural human endeavour.

When the self is properly orientated towards the soul, you can relate and interact appropriately with others. You are spiritually awake and receptive.

Although the genetic background exerts its blueprint upon us, the outer environment also has a considerable impact upon our development and spiritual growth. All human beings are affected by nature and nurture. A neurotic, confused self cannot control the mind and listen to the heart. In these cases patience and special attention, healing and guidance is needed. Self-realisation or gnosis is attained when a union of self and soul is perfected. The enlightened person experiences the world without being confused by events and messages, which flash through the senses upon the mind. Whether the image is that of a stormy ocean or a forest fire, the awakened being neither drowns nor burns with the image. The purified heart is ever still and reflects divine perfection as emitted by the resident soul.

Your inner mirror will benefit by exposure to images and lights from a more perfected mirror, such as a realised teacher.

4.3. FAMILY AND SOCIETY

Personal growth and evolvement occurs due to the interaction between the body, mind, memory, heart and other components of the self, leading it towards self realisation. With two or more people this process is enhanced.

Human beings are social animals who need relationships to evolve and develop to their full potential. Relationships are meaningful when outer differences and diversities are seen through inner similarities. The human love of inner harmony and contentment manifests outwardly in different needs, desires and activities which bring about human togetherness, social inter-action and thereby collective stability.

Every entity in existence transmits messages, which reflect its state and make-up at that time. These communications can be heard by the ear as well as the heart.

The mother's overall state of health during pregnancy has an indelible impact upon the future life of the child. Equally, an attentive upbringing in a supportive and conducive environment gives the child great advantages for future growth and adjustment to people and society. A healthy personality includes emotional stability, rational mentality, ethical conduct, as well as a spiritual reference and guidance. When the person eventually manages to align self and soul, a mature and well-adjusted being is the outcome. The ultimate reference in all of these dynamics is the soul's higher consciousness.

Only unfulfilled parents impose their personal will and expectations upon a child's future career or worldly position.

Every human being has a specific path in growth and evolvement towards self knowledge, which requires sincere intention, serious attention and clarity of direction. The human desire for good company or a partner in life stems from the fact that the self is restless, weak, constantly seeking security and reassurance. Mental limitations and outer habitual actions give the self the illusion that the desired 'soul-mate' is in the outside world and must be acquired. This illusion is one of nature's tricks to 'educate' the self and continue the propagation of the human species. Real spiritual 'education' implies bringing out the light and patterns already etched in the soul.

The self is always looking for acknowledgement and reassuring companionship. This restlessness continues until it realises its true partner is its soul within the heart.

The saying, 'Birds of the same feather flock together', applies only partially to human beings. It fits with regard to outer interests, such as sports, music, culture, hobbies etc. As for spiritual evolvement and progress, one needs to break personal habits and norms that reinforce the self and ego. Thus, a good lasting relationship is more likely to be based upon complementarities, rather than similarities. Your best friend is not always the one who makes you laugh.

The habit of the evolved self to care for others reflects of the soul's concern and love for the self. The more you give, the more you are given.

It is not unusual that one's expectations of fulfilment from others is most likely to end up in disappointment. A marriage falls within this general rule if it is based on the illusion that the key to one's happiness lies in someone else's hands. It is true, however, that another person may help the self to grow emotionally and improve in physical, mental habits and attitudes towards a rational and stable level. However, to change undesirable habits or remove mental blocks is a personal responsibility for whoever desires progress. Sexual attraction and intercourse is a great trick of nature to procreate by uniting complementary bodies for a short period. Everything in existence seeks survival and continuity, reproducing the eternal nature of pure consciousness.

A marriage is as good as the ability of each partner to help the other achieve higher self-knowledge and align self to soul.

The ultimate test of a good relationship between human beings is the level, quality and extent of the love that binds them. Love of gardening, mountain climbing, long distance running, and numerous other bonding 'glues' may be instrumental to bind people together for a while but the shelf-life of that 'glue' is limited. However, love for wisdom, beauty, harmony, self-knowledge and spiritual awakening are high quality ingredients of a love which may last a life time. The source of all love is divine and its manifestation is the unconditional love of soul for the self, irrespective of the ego's waywardness.

We all desire love, unity and togetherness with whom we love. The souls are united in essence, for they all carry the hallmark of the supreme consciousness. Selves echo that state and therefore desire worldly 'get togethers.'

A family is the first school where a child learns and develops physical, mental, psychological and social skills, whilst interacting with others. The mother is the first teacher, most influential in building the foundation of a stable character. Qualities of trust, reliability, self-confidence and other positive, as well as negative, traits are seeded during the first few months of a baby's life. A mother's attention and availability is crucial during this early period. The father's participation grows in importance with the child's mental development and the emergence of the capacity to reason. The feeling of security and safety that the family gives the growing child is crucial to healthy future growth. It is helpful to encourage a child's natural love of fantasy, mythology and fairy tales, as these activities enhance the imaginal capacity of the child, which are preludes to future explorations, discoveries and openings to higher consciousness. A child's behaviour will often reflect aspects of parental traits and states. If the patterns mirrored are negative ones, they may incur the parent's disapproval (unjustly!), whereas positive behaviour that confirms the parent's value systems will earn approval.

If you deny your biological and family origin, your life's journey towards your spiritual origin will be confused and difficult. Hypocrisy and denials are obstacles to discrimination.

The wholesomeness of a family is based on the quality of the parent's love, loyalty and compatibility with each other, as well as the condition of the immediate social, cultural and economic setting to which the family belongs. The child grows to reflect both family and society's prevailing culture. It is not unusual for the weak or sick child in a family to receive more attention than the healthy one. Earthly care for the body and health often takes precedence over caring for higher qualities. A healthy person is one who has a sound body, clear mind and a pure heart which enables the soul to shine through. The same measures apply to a healthy family or society. Social justice, racial and religious tolerance and freedom, equal opportunity for all, a good standard of health and education, social welfare support systems and safety nets are all necessary conditions for a cohesive and stable community.

An apple does not fall too far from its tree. The taste of the fruit relates to the soil, water and climate where it grew. So are the qualities of a child.

The conduct, values and motives of individual behaviour also influences and affects families, societies and sometimes further afield. The human individual is a microcosm containing both the meaning and function of all that appears in groups or nations. The extent of the individual's value system, well-being and evolved consciousness is often a reflection of other people and the macrocosm. Human beings rarely exist in total isolation, even in extreme cases. If you study a few persons selected from across the spectrum of a society, you will most probably be able to form a representative view of that society.

A person's companions and friends exert greater influence upon one than is realised. Like a chameleon, the self takes on the colour of what is close to it.

The human microcosm is like a city with all the features and functions of geographic, socio-economic and political domain. The human organs, senses, anatomy, physiology and psychology echo the society's state at all its levels. Personal health implies efficient and harmonious interaction of all the numerous functions. Similarly, a society's health is a function of its standard of health, education, religion, economy, safety, welfare, cohesiveness and the solidarity of its members and its judicious and other socio-political systems and norms. Another important factor is continuity in collective behaviour, values and traditions. These enhance stability, harmony and well-being.

Knowledge of interconnectedness brings the self closer to the source of the unifying power in life –divine supreme consciousness.

In economically developed societies, issues of formal employment, health, education, retirement, old-age, preparation for death and other personal and community questions play an important role in personal and family welfare. The need for a belief or spiritual path becomes important with old age, for ease of passage and reconciliation with death. Social cohesion, loyalties, interdependence, respect for law, faith, trust of the political, administrative and judicious systems, all play crucial parts in the overall state of contentment and efficient living of people.

Whoever remembers death frequently, before it is due, will be at ease when its time comes. Live the present fully with awareness of the future and end of this journey.

In the social arena we observe the same grid of dualities involving meaning and form, earthly and heavenly, inner and outer. An angry person who shouts (form) and is enraged (meaning) is similar to a nation on the brink of war with its neighbour, which is being accused of violating its borders. National anthems and pageantry too are outer forms reflecting symbols of pride, honour and strength. Personal modesty, wisdom, self-knowledge and accountability are the equivalent of a society that is transparent in its activities, upholds ethical conduct at all levels, welcomes criticism and honours freedom of expression and social justice.

Societies are like the individual self: they have their level of physical, mental and spiritual growth, evolvement, progress and decline.

Personal character develops over the years as a result of inter-action with other people and cultures. The same dynamics applies to a society established in its traditions and norms. Culture, language, customs and other habits define the personality of a society. Leadership, laws, cultural norms, arts, rituals, religious practices and other traditions distinguish different people living in diverse geographic and climatic environments. The way of life, values and customs of desert nomads are very different to that of peasant settlements alongside a river. History, geography, economics, trade and other components of living, reveal much about a people and the character of a nation.

As the outer is never separate from the inner, and each depends upon the other, with insight one sees the intricate connection and inseparability.

Nations and tribes are the natural outcome of extended families and the human quest for a more secure, efficient and sustainable life. Specialisation and exchange of ideas and products between people are also a natural outcome of the human desire for material progress and economical production. The driving force to satisfy needs follows a natural hierarchy, ranging from security, safety and preservation of life, to attaining comfort and ease in day-to-day living. Just as there is the journey of the individual self, societies, tribes and nations too have their natural progress, growths and cycles. When adequate physical or material satisfaction is achieved, then mental, artistic, social aspirations and creativity appear. The need for health and stable relationships are both specific, as well as continuous, whereas many other needs are occasional, such as fighting against an epidemic or an enemy.

The collective self or a national mood follows a similar pattern to the individual self but with less predictable outcome.

The effect of collective consciousness and 'social values' upon an individual's behaviour is considerable at all times. A person may appreciate and practice humility but as a chief of a tribe or head of a state, humility may be considered a weakness. Thus you observe double standards. A confused society may head for a great tragedy, whereas a disturbed individual can only cause limited damage. In a quarrel or physical fight there are often two levels of intentions: one is to subdue and bring into line the adversary, such as a father who shakes a wayward son to bring him to attention; the other level is to destroy and shatter the enemy with total brutality and no hope for reconciliation. Both of these situations often occur in societies and in world politics.

The root of all discord and chaos is the lack of alignment between personal and soul consciousness, both on the micro level (individual), as well as on the macro level (societal).

'Normal' often means familiar, customary and habitual and, therefore, predictable and understandable in a cultural sense. Most individual human beings consider themselves normal, while aspiring to be super or supra-normal. The implication is that even though we may have much in common with each other, individually and collectively we desire to excel above others and be recognized as special and distinguished. This natural tendency reveals the truth that every human soul is intrinsically special and perfect, whereas every person's merit is gauged according to personal skills, talents and other human abilities and competence. Many individuals, families, tribes, nations or religious groups consider themselves as favoured by god as 'chosen people'. This reflects the truth that every soul is god-chosen and has an inner programme for enabling the self to unfold to its divine potential. The self, however, needs to yield to the soul in order to be content and happy.

The desire of the self to share outer experiences with others is a reflection of the shared sameness of all souls. In essence, all human beings are the same in spiritual potential.

With regards to the direction and purpose in life, what applies to the human individual also applies to families, societies and nations. We all desire to reach and maintain an optimum condition in survival, strength, stability, contentment and spiritual awakening. Our present world differs from the past (in backdrops), as well as being similar (in essential motives). This is always the case. Some new factors of values, ethics and lifestyle are drastically different from the recent past. Global information technologies and human mobility will affect all societies, families and individuals to varying degrees and with ever increasing speed and force. The challenges are great if one desires to maintain spiritual goals without abandoning cultural values and familiar social habits.

Personal values and state of consciousness can change much easier than that of a society or community. Cultural habits, religion and traditions are comforting partly due to the habit of continuity and illusion of security due to familiarity.

4.4. CIVILISATIONS AND CULTURES

A culture gives security and satisfies an aspect of the self's need to belong. The socio-cultural mindset is much more resilient and durable than the individual's mind.

Within every society there are diverse strands of relationships based on social, cultural, economic, ethnic, religious and other social bonds and connections. These are the basic ingredients of a discernable culture. A society's interest in economics, arts, science, politics, philosophy, spirituality and other issues describe the state and vitality of its people. The religious and spiritual orientation reflect the extent of its interest in meaning and purpose in life in a society. A nation devoid of interest in higher ethics or morality will invariably decline and disintegrate. The state of an individual or a nation clearly discerned by the astute observer, through considering routine habits, daily activities, socio-economic relationships and other factors of communal character.

To know the real state of a man or a nation, listen with your heart to their sounds and sights, leisure activities and their relationship with death.

The social mindset is conservative and desires conventional stability and continuity. Individuals and societies look for reinforcement and confirmation of their cultural values, habits and practices. This is a natural way for people to find social fulfilment and security within the protective feeling of group solidarity, based on love of the familiar. It is natural to reinforce existing norms, habits and traditions within the group context. Relationships operate like interactive mirrors between individuals, as well as between diverse strands within society.

Minority group interests can disproportionately influence the majority towards changes in values and customs. An enlightened self may be a 'one-off' in a group but can certainly exert strong influence towards higher values. Equally, a degenerate, manic person could adversely affect group behaviour.

The outer state of a person or a society reveals much of its inner. The two states reflect, resonate with and reinforce each other.

Civilised life is founded as a network of norms and customs amongst a community of people who are connected by proximity, language, religion, race and other factors. A civilisation develops its identity based on accepted cultural norms. Rigid cultural values and intolerance curtail both an individual's and society's creative growth and healthy responses to new challenges. A dynamic individual, seeking fulfilment, needs a culture that offers the right environment for creative personal growth. The concern of modern nations with the 'brain drain/gain' is a clear appreciation of the human 'knowledge' capital. Successful nations maintain a flexible mainstream culture while confidently accepting and assimilating new minds, without fear of loss of the old norms. A vibrant nation has no fear of its old habits being diluted or changed. It lives confidently in the present with positive aspirations for the future, whilst holding fast to fairness and justice.

The more there is inner security and stability, the less there will be fear or concern regarding outer power and unwanted influences.

An individual has an ego, virtues and vices, as does a society. An individual may perceive the wisdom of humility, but with the collective ego, issues of social perception, acceptability and status are reinforced by the traditional norms. Hypocrisy or double standards manifest when people respect power and authority but resent it being applied to them. Many nations love the identity of the eagles on their flags but would like to be honoured and respected internationally as doves or peace-lovers.

Personal inadequacy, weakness and confusion are often reflected in a community or society with greater complexity and is difficult to correct.

The fear and lack of understanding of death causes much pain and agony for individuals, as well as for families and societies. For an enlightened person, death is a natural and welcome transformation. Owing to the self's identification with the body, the mind produces the emotion of suffering loss through death. In a dying person, fear is mostly due to facing the unknown. In a society, however, grief, suffering and loss after natural or other disasters become magnified in the collective mind. There is a major difference between a society where a cemetery is regarded as barren ground to express sadness and grief, to those who see it as a pleasant park, where souls take off to a subtler realm.

Everything within the ocean of existence has a beginning and an end, but the ocean itself is eternal. This is why the self longs for immortality.

Due to spiritual ignorance, the relentless pursuit of outer material possessions results in suffering from inner insecurity and impoverishment. The richer nations have not succeeded in eradicating outer poverty, owing to their failure to promote qualities of sharing, selflessness, inner contentment and a simple way of living. The constant desire to consume and 'get' things does not leave much energy or space for the self to realise that it has itself already been 'got' by its joyful soul. To realise this inner occupation one needs to be least concerned for being outwardly occupied.

The welfare state can stifle individual initiatives, though it may relieve many people from stifling material poverty and even possible criminal acts.

Nations in the West are the offspring of the historical renaissance, reformation movements and a huge industrial revolution. They have grown up on a diet of responsible freedom and a quest for outer excellence in a competitive environment. They enjoy evolving work ethics and values, within stable political and cultural set-ups. The effect of geography, weather, strategic positions and other factors are always important considerations in shaping a people's economic and national development. When Indians or Africans, who were considered lazy at home, were removed from their harsh and debilitating environments to European climes, their productivity did not lag behind their western counterparts. Human beings are much influenced by the outer climate and social environment, irrespective of past cultural, geographical or racial origins.

You cannot but adopt and accept, to a certain extent, the ways of the people you work and live with. As with the air we breathe we are influenced by what is close at hand.

In placing events and experiences into categories and hierarchies and ascribing a value and importance to them language is curcial. When one labels and organises something it ceases to live and evolve naturally, for whatever is alive is subject to constant incremental change. No quality can be fixed by name or strictly defined for any duration. At a personal as well as societal level mental conditioning and rigidity are great obstacles to inner mobility and spiritual progress. Oral traditions can communicate spiritual states easier than written languages and cultures.

If every endeavour is reduced to rationality and reasoning we shall end up with a dull grey world, replete with futile pursuits and frivolous pleasures – standardised and justified.

The natural human quest for self-knowledge and discovery of the inner world has been repeatedly described by numerous religious teachings, enlightened prophets and messengers. One's religion is often an accident of birth and attempts to make sense with what is experienced between birth and death. Religion in a society can increase solidarity when it is pliant and fresh, but can cause breaches and divisions when structured and organised. The downside to religion is the rigidity of institutionalised habits and rituals, which often overshadow the original meaning, spirit and transformative purpose. Structures also produce a class of clergy or theocrats, who exercise worldly power based on assumed divine authority. Religious history is often written to please those seeking increased reassurance in what they already believe in and their particular delusions.

A religion without practice cannot lead to spiritual development. A ritual without a clear religious meaning and philosophy is an absurd theatre.

Worship *of* the altar is often a more common practice than worship *at* the altar. Some religious people have replaced love, knowledge and worship of god, which is only meaningful through his attributes and qualities, with obsessive glorification of the religion itself and its historical rituals. In this process religion is often stripped of its transformative meaning, thus reinforcing institutionalised dogmas and creed. Evolved members of a religion may rediscover the more universal spiritual content of their belief and reconcile by uplifting and adopting some of the inherited practices and commonly accepted ideas. 'Reborn' Christians, Muslims, Hindus or others, often rediscover transformative aspects of their religion and are revitalised and excited by this renewal.

When truly lived, a religion can elevate and transform, and can deform when forced and elevated beyond grasp. God honours the most humble and those who serve creation best.

In some western countries, national, cultural, political and economic integration were often cornerstones in establishing a civil society and a patriotic nation. Elsewhere, whenever a racial or ethnic group asserted its rule, the result was often disorder and bloodshed. Generally, no human being, tribe, society or nation considers itself as inferior to others. The deep root of this pride is the human soul, which is the most sublime and superior entity in the whole of creation. Higher evolvement implies the self's awareness of its inadequacy and egotism. Self-sacrifice and death for a legitimate communal cause is considered heroic and admired by all cultures. It is a reflection of the subconscious truth of the insignificance of the self and immortality of the soul. When a community commemorates a hero, they are in truth upholding the truth of the soul's immortality and transiencey of the self.

A civil society flourishes upon individual respect, equal opportunity and tolerance of diverse people. Intolerance is often due to fears and other insecurities.

The social paradox of admiring a real self-sacrificing hero, as well as the denounced. The pretentious or self serving hero, is because the human being is composed of both a perfect soul and its ego shadow. One is durable and is to be acknowledged, the other is to be denounced and rejected. Whoever lives the life of a soul is admired and whoever cares for the self and its images is denounced.

The self's tendency to hero worship relates to its seeking of perfection. Yet no self is ever perfect, for that quality belongs to the soul.

'Primitive' societies lived very simply in deep awareness of their environment and would respond sensitively to outer changes and signs. Contemporary societies have replaced these subtle senses with modern technology, increased material dependence and complicated social habits, which we label as progress and civilisation. Celebration of birthdays, anniversaries, national events, honouring heroes, manners of dress, eating habits, flags and displayed achievements are all part of superficial cultural baggage. If we aspire to attain a higher level of consciousness collectively, then we need to worship god through the individual and collective souls and give that endeavour priority in our life.

In many ancient religious cultures, idols or gods often symbolised aspects of divine attributes and represented human longing and desires for these qualities.

Human needs and desires can never be fulfilled for at no time will the self be totally content. Real self-fulfilment is based upon the discovery of the inner soul-mate and thereby the attainment of lasting security. In the same way, the material or outer progress of a nation cannot be fulfilling, unless it is paralleled by spiritual evolvement. Outer, as well as inner, poverty needs to be addressed at the same time, otherwise the results will be an imbalanced life and discontentment. Like everything else in creation, poverty has two dimensions, and ignoring this dualism is a common and foolish oversight. It is easier to eradicate either outer or inner poverty, but not both at the same time.

Fearless courage simply reflects the self's desire to go beyond limitations, norms and mediocrity. The soul's courage is boundless and the ignorant self imitates blindly.

Virtues such as generosity, patience and tolerance of others are generally accepted and universally desired but the ways in which these qualities are practiced differ. Most people desire to love and be loved but are ignorant of the nature of love and its unconditional divine origin. True love is when you regard others as yourself in essence and enjoy outer differences. Equally so, differences in a society are easier to reconcile by reference to the sameness of the sacred source of life within every member.

The deep human sense of fairness and justice supersedes all logic.

Religious judgement regarding 'good' or 'evil' often has its roots in historical animosities, misunderstanding and ignorance based on egotism. What appears to be religious conflict is often simply human discord, based on ignorance, greed and other worldly vices. There has often been more killings between sects of a specific religion than between those of differing faiths. There is a tendency for people to use religion as an excuse to reinforce an idea or prejudice, which relates to the lower self and the insecure, fearful and neurotic ego. When the rational self is not strong and the spiritual connection between head and heart is not established, bizarre actions are justified irrationally. This is how a normal 'good' person can commit acts of violence or crime in the name of religion or god! Also, this heartless self receives reinforcing signals from others with similar confused waywardness.

A religion followed with sincerity, devotion and humility can help the self to evolve; otherwise it will increase devaluation and degradation of the self.

From time immemorial, human beings have always looked to the supernatural to enhance faith and belief. This is a natural reflection of the boundless mysterious soul within us. The development of religion and the priestly class of intermediaries is an understandable historical occurrence, due to the variation in people's capacity for knowledge and ability to think and act responsibly and independently. Throughout human history there have been pragmatic alliances between worldly rulers who wished to rule over people's bodies, with religious leaders who wished to rule over minds or souls. As a result, the earthly rulers used guns and violence, while the priesthood promised punishment or rewards in the hereafter. Institutionalised religions often endured because of the symbiotic relationship between such rulers and theologians and the sense of continuity and cohesion a religion gives its people. Ethics and moral codes regarding respect and preservation of life are accepted by most religions and societies. Reverence for human life reflects the universal love of the creator of the soul and the giver of life.

To follow and live a religion sincerely can be an important stabilising element in the life of a person and society. Equally, deep seated dogmas can cause much communal suffering.

It is often said that a prophet is denounced by his own people. Generally, truth and divine light are considered to be far away in the heavens above or in some future time. Familiarity often breeds contempt; for this reason kings and rulers often created a wide distance between themselves and the public. They were thus able to maintain an air of magisterial mystery and even divinity. It is said that two sufis can peacefully share a small mattress but two kings will not be content to divide a country between them. Greed and egotistical self-esteem are major barriers to personal and societal spiritual progress.

When worldly kings become the 'defenders of the faith', much of that faith will be controlled by world finance, industry, politics and modern-day fiefdoms of corporations.

Present day democracies are based on the adoption of pluralism, yet the world's economic and political drives are fuelled by selfish monopolistic ambitions, reinforced by science, technology, and universal industrial, political and financial systems that reinforce each other. Communism was a futile attempt to force earthly human beings to stop caring about personal worldly possessions and power in the name of an illusory socialist or collective god. Unless the self gives in to the soul's perfections voluntarily, its obsessions with possessions will not be forcibly neutralized or transcended. It is always easy to distract people from pursuing human potential and spiritual awakening; it is difficult to popularise modesty, abstention and the bliss of peaceful meditation and silent prayer.

It is foolish to expect divine justice on earth without having exercised human responsibility, accountability, personal and social justice.

With wisdom and old age one perceives a wider and deeper decadence and corruption everywhere. This is partly why many zealous people predict the end of time or the advent of a messiah. Also, the wiser one gets, the wider and deeper will grow the field of one's consciousness. Thus, one sees more faults and misdeeds than is possible with the narrower horizon of youth. So it is natural for a person to be more despondent with age, unless it is balanced with spiritual insight and understanding. An aging person naturally grows more rigid physically but with that comes the potential compensation of a flexible mind and a living, overflowing heart. When one meets an old person with an awakened heart, the cheerfulness on the face betrays the inner youthfulness in contrast with physical age.

Worldly or physical losses or constrictions can be more than compensated for by gains in spiritual wisdom and joy.

We train our children in aggressive competition and acquisition, whilst expecting their respectful cooperation, kindness and consideration. We forcefully teach them the skills and ways of the outer world with little education about the inner world and care for the heart. This imbalance is mostly due to the fact that the outer world is easier to understand and tackle. It is the world of the heart and the soul that is elusive: to know it one needs to learn from those who have already developed this science for themselves and applied it with discipline and determination. We need to apply the teaching fully before experiencing transformation.

Human rights are meaningful after exercising human responsibility; transformative spirituality follows authentic humanity.

Excessive watering of plants causes the roots to rot and also impedes the flowering and bearing of fruit. Similarly with human beings: excessive concern and protection inhibits the natural process of a child's maturity, self responsibility, resilience and other life skills. The same principle applies to society when it weakens, due to lack of stimulating challenges and the presence of an over-protective welfare state which inhibits adaptability and striving. Excesses and luxurious ways are signs of weaknesses in a culture and symptoms of decadence. One redeeming feature of the modern residential boarding school is that the student learns the value of sharing with and caring for others and that no-one can keep a secret for long. Children are cruelly clever in exposing their peers' quirks.

Entertainment and sports are well expressed in old French as 'disport', which means 'distract' or 'amuse'. They can distract and lead to a disproportionate sense of values.

The failure of a society is often due to ignorant, incompetent or arrogant political leadership, sometimes reinforced by suspect religious personalities. Human love of status and self importance will naturally bring about, in time, its well deserved opposite of dishonour and humility. The effective leader is like a gardener, judiciously safeguarding all aspects of his garden by weeding, watering and pruning. Good leadership brings about gradual change, compatible with what is naturally sustainable, where individuals' freedoms, rights and accountability are upheld, and a respected system of justice is practiced effectively. Internal differences need to be brought to the surface without being suppressed, and to be addressed with impartial seriousness, then dealt with justly and openly. Nothing can be imposed for a long time upon people without their acceptance of it. During times of difficulty, people want to have a reliable leader they can trust. During times of relative ease, successful politicians are those who echo the desires of the masses. Thus, the profile of successful leadership differs according to the nature of the times.

A great leader does not claim privilege and authority but acknowledges duty and responsibility, regarding himself as dispensable.

Conditioned consciousness covers a wide range of the self's qualities, such as the childish irresponsible self, the totalitarian despotic self, the emotional self, the reasonable but weak self, the rational self and others, up to the wise and awakened self. The same sort of spectrum applies to political leaders and national heroes or icons. The different selves rule over a person as different leaders over a nation or a country. If you study the psyche of great historical leaders you can see that most of their wars and actions were reflections of their evolving or devolving selves at that time and those circumstances. They did not make history – they simply acted it out on the gross outer stage of life.

As the person is, the self rules over it; as the nation is, its leaders connect and fit with their aspirations and desires. Think of mirrors.

Contrary to popular claims, the extent of conflicts in the world is surprisingly low at both personal and societal levels! It is indeed a miracle that there is peace at all, given the natural neurotic, confused and erratic state of the self with its egotistical tendencies. In a world where the quest for supreme consciousness is replaced with money or power it is no wonder that strife and poverty is so pervasive both outwardly and inwardly. No wonder the angels in heaven were shocked when god created Adam, as the story goes, giving him apparent freedom of choice. But god also placed the sacred soul in Adam's heart for guidance.

The outer conduct or state of a person or society is a good indication of the inner state of the individual or the nation. The inner and outer always reflect each other.

The divine right of kings has its deep origin in the natural human desire for loyalty, responsibility and acceptance of subjugation by the king who truly represents god on earth as a steward. Only sincere and transparent accountability to higher values can qualify a person to witness divine mercy and compassion in the transient and ever-changing world. It is only when one lives in gratitude for the generosity of the creator and has a deep respect for other creations that one can exercise real compassion, patience, goodwill and love.

Whoever desires to rule is not fit to rule. Indeed, all rights are the natural outcome of responsibilities. Desire to rule is only justified when it becomes desire to serve and is accepted as such.

At the moment we are unable to assess the effect of the revolutionary changes that have taken place in the information and knowledge industries. Early in the twentieth century a major shift from agrarian life to industrial ways and methods took place in the western world. This was due to the common availability of the internal combustion engine and fossil based energy which ushered in a change of life and work with worldwide implications. Today's 'knowledge' workers are self-supervising, networking and performing more efficiently through 'connectivity' processes involved in their daily work duties or contracts. The future world's digital library will make research and 'finding out' more universal and accessible. These new openings will produce quantum changes in everyone's life.

A good leader is steady in behaviour, reliable and cheerful both when in power and when out of it. Such a leader is primarily led by his/her own heart and soul.

No country or society can ignore the new global forces at work. However, the outcome could be both beneficial, as well as detrimental, depending on people's outlook on life and the meaning and purpose they give to it. If we care for sharing goodness with others, then globalisation and the information revolution are welcome and 'god-sent'. In truth, everything in existence is god-sent but we need to read the message correctly and respond appropriately. Satan is also god's creation. The key issue is what is appropriate and to what end. If it is to realise, both individually and collectively, the importance of balancing inner and outer realities and needs, then we are heading towards a healthy and fruitful global evolvement. Otherwise, we will collectively suffer from a diminished world of suffocating brutality: a materially-efficient global village without the open spaces, village green and celebration of life; an industrial park with plastic flowers and plants visited by unhappy and overstressed people. A virtual nightmare.

The quality of one's life is as good as the balance of inner and outer realities – the ultimate reference being the constant truth that lies within and beyond existence.

The new global culture will naturally encourage all people to fit into the ruling equation of global supply and demand as regulated by semi-monopolies and faceless corporations. Thus, in terms of knowledge, skills and even survival, there are now dominant economic indications and measures which no nation can avoid. Those who defy the new avalanche of 'scientifically' proven rules and measures will be marginalised to below subsistence living.

In a global village you cannot be safe (let alone be happy) with half the village hungry and deprived.

The future of the world in the short-term is firmly charted by the new megalithic, corporate, multinational powers and the dominant hard-line materialist mindset. The explosive information revolution is energised by the dynamics of connecting opposites, which is the foundation of the binary system. The semiconductor is a kind of middle material between conductors and insulators, where a 'barrier field' can be created to control the flow of electrons. The irony is that sand is the most abundant material on earth and the silicon chip, which is made from it, is now at the centre of global human activities. What will come as a new surprise is the global thirst for the discovery of that which is nearer to us than 'nearness' itself: the light in the heart and pure consciousness.

Any entity in existence which goes beyond its limit reverts to its opposite.

The promise of instant outer access and connection is a reflection of what is already within each human being – the ever present connection between mind and heart, self and soul. Success in outer business is a minor reflection of the self's access to the ever victorious soul. We are inherently seekers of heavenly joy but distracted by shadowy ghosts of earthly pleasure. The live-now-pay-later ethos of the credit card with its glittering promises of instant satisfaction is based upon the human self's inability to accept limitation and conditionality. The entire growth of world trade is based on the self's desires to acquire the soul's boundless treasures. Another facet of this false promise is the huge industry for gambling, where the self desires instant wealth, mimicking the soul's access to everything and need of nothing. Once the self submits to the soul, the result is harmony and peace both for the person and society. However, this theory needs to be translated into strategies and plans by individuals and societies who desire the spiritual way of life on earth. It is difficult to think about. It needs to be tasted by inner resolve for awakening to truth.

In our present society many people consider themselves free. How can you be free when you have self-concern, self-image and fear of death?

5. INFORMATION AND TRANSFORMATION

Human growth and evolvement is enhanced as we respond to facts and information by reference to rationality as well as higher consciousness.

Personal consciousness evolves when the senses, mind and body interact with the outer world and 'make sense' out of events and situations. The mind develops by investigating cause and effect, and the connection between new experiences and events with past memory and knowledge. The self needs to exchange news and information, transmit and receive feelings and evaluations, in order to evolve further in consciousness. The human urge to push the boundaries of possibilities further into the unknown is constant. The 'sky is the limit' is a natural human tendency, for we are both earthly (limited in personal consciousness) and heavenly (boundless pure consciousness). Thus, the sky is not the limit; it is the prelude to higher and endless 'skies'.

Today's vast quantities of available information present a challenge and opportunity as to how best to utilise this wealth of data and information for the sake of inner transformation. Transformation implies transcending self images, the rational mind and the discernable world towards pure consciousness, beyond all specific, tangible realities and experience. This drive motivates the search for perfection in all worldly situations but it is frustrating at the same time, for our natural world is subject to change and unpredictability. Thus we seek perfection always (where the state of the soul is) and can never attain it for any duration.

Personal suffering is the result of distractions in the self's hesitant progress towards inner realisation, fulfilment and contentment. The self always desires states and experiences that are not realistic or sustainable in the changing world of space-time. Every self innately aspires for the qualities of the soul and thus can only be content after submitting to the soul's boundless light and high consciousness. Freedom, as such, is a by-product of unity between the head and heart, self and soul. The soul is ever free and the self is ever restless in its search.

It is a wise one who is always hopeful to learn meanings and lessons from difficulties and hardships.

5.1. SUFFERING AND OFFERINGS

God does not mete out punishment. It is the ignorant self and its wrong actions that bring grief and sorrow, as a warning against distractions, the lack of inner reference and harmony.

The worldly suffering, cruelty and injustices are for us human beings to object to and eradicate as they are due to our own action in the first place. This world is like god's nursery and we are growing up minute by minute until we pierce the veils of time and act as the connecting point between that which is finite and infinity.

Mistakes, failures, obsessions, addictions and expectations are some of the reasons given for human suffering. Only when personal consciousness is aligned to soul consciousness will we experience harmony, contentment and well-being. The self was designed to seek union with its inner soulmate but due to outer distractions it deviates from its intended destiny and suffers as a consequence. These mistakes are in fact part of one's learning process and growing up. We have at all times the mental and spiritual capacity to find solutions to the problems we create for ourselves, otherwise hope and trust are meaningless.

Every human suffering has its root in self-deception, ignorance and mental illusions. The diligent seeker regards failures and difficulties as messages prompting one to take corrective steps with greater self awareness and accountability.

Suffering implies discordance, difficulties, disconnectedness, disharmony and the lack of unity of consciousness. The mind cannot relate the event or experience with past images and values satisfactorily. Some people may consider suffering as god's punishment, whereas in truth god is the source of all creation and consciousness, good or bad. The self is designed to fear suffering and pain, in order to survive in body and mind and evolve further. Human suffering is a warning signal of the discord between intended or expected outcome and actual experience.

All suffering is a painful reminder of the need for greater attention, care and knowledge inwardly as well as outwardly. Pain is a natural helpful warning that is turned into suffering by the emotional mind.

Human beings are always distressed by suffering and discord and continuously desire harmony and balance. Perception of good and bad differs according to one's inner state as it relates to outer circumstances and events. Cutting off a finger accidentally is dreadful but a surgeon's scalpel removing a crushed finger is a welcome act of kindness to preserve the arm. It may be a painful operation but a necessary one in view of the bigger picture. It is the rational mind and spiritual insight that can reduce or override suffering and other negative emotions.

All values and judgements are relative and change according to context and association.

Feelings are personal mental responses to outer events or situations. Soul consciousness energises personal consciousness which, through the senses, memories and values, produces feelings. When the senses signal a situation or an event contradicting a desire or expectation, the stressed mind expresses anger, disappointment, fear, aggression or other emotions. Positive emotions result when outer events match with our expected outcome. Reflecting upon one's emotions while referring to higher consciousness can lead to new insights and connections between the self and soul consciousness. Empathy or sympathy with another person's suffering occurs by transposing the discordant emotions or the pain of the other person onto one's own mind to reproduce a similar feeling or state.

The self naturally picks up an aspect of other people's grief and is affected positively or negatively to a certain degree. It also can feel gratitude for being spared that particular suffering itself. Survival and self protection always play their role.

We generally regard suffering as an undesirable state and we put up with pain in the hope of future improvement. Contentment and harmony is a narrow path safeguarded by the barriers, which have pain and warning inscribed on all sides. The origin of negative emotions (anger, fear, distress etc) is based on the primal urge to know and be free from all personal limitations. Perfection is at the root of whatever there is in existence but to hear its subtle whispers requires a gnostic's ear. People who serve in disasters and refugee camps are uplifted by seeing others who are in pain. To help alleviating other people's pain takes one beyond one's own suffering threshold.

Fear relates to the possible absence of what is available now at some future time. We fear loss of a good job, failing memory and poor health.

The metaphor of Adam and Eve in the perpetual bliss of the garden implies constant cognizance of perfection before changing states or space-time. The great vistas of knowledge and perfection were not discernable in this heavenly abode because ignorance and faults had not yet been experienced. Paradise could not be appreciated and earned until hell was experienced and avoided. The devil or satan is like pain and sorrow: a creation to be guarded against if we are to escape black holes and destruction. Yet, even satan can be a beneficial signpost along our spiritual journey if we interpret the message properly, which is a warning to turn away. Thus, mankind had to evolve through learning about earthly limitation, need, and through outer experiences of misery and joy and all other polarities.

Circles of fire protect paradise from unqualified intruders while hell is camouflaged by enticing gardens and distracting sites.

The root of all suffering, sadness, grief and disappointment lies in the discrepancy between the actual event and what the self has desired or expected. If the disappointing event is viewed with rationality and reference to pure consciousness, then the painful mental shadow will dissolve through the light of the truth and fact of the situation. Suffering arises from the denial or rejection of an occurrence and the assignment of an emotional value to that event. This mental state produces self pity and ego entrapment. When the self puts on a brave face in an accident it is reflecting an aspect of the 'ever-perfect' soul. This is how pain is sometimes overlaid by higher consciousness. This is the wisdom of appropriate response to events with mind and heart.

Crises and disasters are opportunities for the self to review the quality of its mind and purity of heart. Every difficulty is an opportunity for an improved adjustment at head and heart.

Collective values are reinforced and magnified by people with similar views. A culture of superiority or victimhood is difficult to change or modify without considerable social disturbance. Human injustice and abuse can afflict a whole people, including the innocents who happened to be in the 'wrong' place at the 'wrong' time. Conflict and pain are unavoidable in a world of change. The sorrow and suffering of today are not the same as yesterday. People's view of pleasure or pain vary according to time and place. But at all times everyone welcomes the reassurance that the future will be better.

When thoughts, images and emotions become trapped in the mind they reinforce the ego and the lower self.

Human evolvement, individually and collectively, occurs by progress from conditioned consciousness to higher consciousness and the dissolution of personal difficulties into insignificance. When faced with calamities and disasters, the self will either rise in consciousness towards the soul, or sink into dark egotistical tunnels and cul-de-sacs. The same pattern relates to a community or society. They can act selflessly, with magnanimity and valour, or get caught up with sorrow, pain and self pity.

Even when one accepts responsibility for one's actions, the outcome is not always as expected. The challenge is to see perfection irrespective of our personal feelings or expectations.

The individual and collective human drive towards perfection is a fundamental force in life, often described as love for excellence or success. However, when this drive is directed towards outer wealth, power or pleasure, without the counter-balance of spiritual content, new discords emerge. Love of money, for example, will bring about additional concerns that increase in proportion to the increase in income. Our present day pursuits of corporately managed mega events in sport, tourism and other leisure activities cannot be sustained without greater cost and damage to the quality of human life and our fragile habitat.

The inner meaning of all suffering is deviation from life's purpose of evolvement in consciousness through experiencing modesty and kindness to others.

Aging and death are topics most people prefer not to discuss; and there is a tendency to postpone reconciliation with these inevitable events. Acceptance of death is generally easier for those who believe in life after death than for those who have no religious belief or spiritual interest. At all times the mind and the self seek durability and eternity, which are qualities of the soul and not the self. The body, however, will age and die and the person's conditioned consciousness along with its soul will move to the non space-time zone of the hereafter. With old age one's eyesight may weaken but it can be more than compensated with greater wisdom and insight. Life is a journey from ignorance and worldly illusion to higher awareness and knowledge – from self to soul.

When a person remains identified with the mind and the body, death is a dreadful event. For the self that is in unison with the soul, death is a natural relief and freedom from earthly limitations.

In nature, life and death are always interacting and connected. Yet, to the human mind they appear as conflicting opposites. Mini births and deaths occur simultaneously and at every moment in life, when the past vanishes and new future is born. Birth denies the past and death denies the future, for both past and the future are absent at those moments. Fear of death is due to the mind and its anxiety about the unknown future. For an enlightened person, death is a simple transition from the world of space-time to other realms. The more one has practised meditation and transcendence from the world of forms to meanings and essence, the easier the actual final event will be. The more the self is attached to physical forms and has identified with them, the more resistant it will be for departure into the unknown.

Desire for, or fear of, death implies a lack of witnessing present perfection. This is due to the veils between the self and the soul.

In sickness the 'dis-ease' can be reduced or reversed if the patient embraces 'ease' and considers the pain as part of a process towards an eventual cure. The immune system is always enhanced by cheerfulness and hope. A light-hearted and positive attitude is known to help hormones to produce the appropriate body chemistry. A flexible and relaxed attitude will give the self a better chance of alignment with the heart and soul. However, as the lower self finds comfort and security in routine habits and what is familiar from the past, sickness too can become habitual. The childish mind gets stuck in its emotions and stubbornly justifies itself. Unless the mind evolves to the rational state it remains confused, sick and blames bad luck or other excesses.

You will overcome illness and disease quicker if your mind is at peace and your thoughts are positive and pleasant. More important than the actual event is your attitude and correct interpretation of it.

The nature of the human self is not to accept blame or responsibility. Hence, an immature person accuses others when experiencing difficulties, hardship or suffering. The evolved person blames himself, however, for ignorance and lack of wisdom and takes responsibility for what has gone wrong. A difficulty is regarded as a good lesson. Constrictions can lead to new knowledge and openings. The habit of self-pity and psychological suffering is a great handicap in one's life. In order to get out of the case of reinforcing suffering, constant watchfulness of the self's tendency to justify itself whilst blaming others is required.

Witnessing perfection in every event or situation occurs when the person looks though the perfect lens of the soul and its pure consciousness.

To avoid self pity, the self must give up its mindset and expand personal perceptions and consciousness through change in conduct and attitude. When you follow an authentic spiritual path and learn wisdom from more advanced beings, your progress will speed up. Self-knowledge and awareness will be enhanced if you visualise that your teachers and those you respect are present and watching your thoughts, intentions and actions. In truth, you are never alone, so be aware at all times. Your soul knows; so does your self through its heightened consciousness. To get to that state, expose your innermost thoughts to your teachers and guides. This is the road by which we unify self and soul and witness the light of unity within duality.

Outer and inner pains are natural warnings and messages for attention and corrective actions, but our minds label them as suffering, instead of factual events requiring management.

When one has had enough pain and sickness the desire to change from this unacceptable state may bring in the required change. Then with careful reflection one may see the perfection of the causal dynamics which brought about the difficulties and affliction. Only then can real healing begin. There can be no lasting progress without first having a neutral and then a positive attitude.

When you blame others the ego is protected for a while, but if you blame yourself greater wisdom and fresh insights are the rewards.

In truth the nature of the self is ignorance and restlessness. Caution comes into play when one knows that every action has an equivalent reaction, which may appear in a different way to the original action. The wise person endeavours to discipline the self and mind, due to the knowledge that every intention, action or thought will leave behind its repercussion and traces. Nothing in existence is ever lost; the recognition of this profound fact brings about thorough accountability and the need for constant vigilance. The demand of religions for obedience is based on the basic need for the self to be harnessed and restricted in the hope of soul connection at the expense of ego expansion.

Difficulties and constrictions are experienced by the self before inner openings and connections occur between head and heart.

Hope is based on the natural human belief that a situation can be improved. The pain of today is often accompanied by the expectation of relief tomorrow. Hope becomes real and more likely to be realised when one acts with a positive attitude towards an appropriate objective. Most people prefer hopefulness to despondency. The soul transmits rays of hope, whereas the ego exudes dark fear and greed. The ego is a bundle of edited memories restricting the conditioned consciousness from the light of higher consciousness. It is like driving forward whilst looking only in the rear-view mirror. Most of us are sorrowful about the past or overly concerned about the future while reflecting little upon the present. This unhealthy state misses the timeless moment by looking at the future through the past. Neurosis and confusion are the natural outcomes.

God's supreme consciousness emits its universal light to all souls and evolving selves and any evil is simply the dark shadow of this light.

Suffering is due to ignorance or distraction from the primal cause and purpose of life: to be led by soul consciousness so as to realise unconditional joy. The journey to this desirable state begins by avoiding the ego's distractions and pitfalls. When the naturally ungroomed, restless self is frustrated by confusing thoughts and inconsistent and unfulfillable desires, a point of helplessness will eventually be reached. The self is like an emotional child of the soul, which needs to be harnessed and restricted so as to reflect and refer to its master and guide –the soul. This process requires a purified heart where self and soul can meet in unison.

When you recognise your impatience you are at the threshold of patience. In the same way poverty can take you to the door of boundless inner riches. Persevere and you will find yourself on the other side.

Nostalgia for the 'good old days' often arises due to selective memory and emotions which sap one's energy. The best day is now, today, seen through the lens of perfection. The search for friendship, compatible companionship and love in this world is energised by the primal quest of the self to be at one with the eternal soul, thus experiencing durable wellness. When that state is realised, most fears, illusions and other neuroses will disappear or loosen their hold.

Optimism prevails when the self takes on the expansive qualities of the soul. Pessimism results when the self is distracted by its ego and is deprived of the soul's light.

For the self to maintain its trust, positive attitude and high expectation in life, it needs access to soul consciousness, especially after disappointments. Total trust is a quality of the soul. The self, however, has limited knowledge and light due to the conditioning of personal consciousness. The soul on the other hand reflects divine light, which is the fountainhead of all knowledge, and the self evolves towards soul awareness and higher consciousness. The most generous and precious gift in creation is the human soul. Like all special gifts, god has presented it well-packaged and wrapped up in layers of self and mind-sets. To get to the soul each person must remove the numerous veils of the ego by determination, discipline and knowledge of the spiritual path.

Sadness and grief are emotional mental shadows that can only be relieved when the light of higher consciousness chases them away.

Pure consciousness is ever-present within each soul and is the source of life and its code of growth and evolvement. Thus, all sufferings and outer difficulties challenge the self to seek higher references and guidance beyond mind, ego and memory. Pain and pleasure are simply mental messages indicating acceptance or repulsion. Beyond these struggles we seek durable happiness, which is a by-product of self-knowledge and the transcendence of mind and emotions. Without a clear mind and intellect the self is handicapped in this world; yet, with reasoning and rationality alone the self has no real joy. Only when worldly wisdom is complemented by heavenly light can a person attain balance, harmony and unison between the outer and inner worlds. This state occurs when self and soul are at one.

Happiness is a by-product of accepting the present, whilst striving for a more illumined future. Spiritual wisdom will ultimately reveal that the present moment was always there without past or future.

By witnessing perfection you place yourself at the meeting point of the two domains of the seen and unseen, form and meaning, the inner and outer, the earthly and heavenly. Your mind is conscious of new perceptions and experiences, whereas the heart and soul transmit pure consciousness and the patterns of permanent truth. Miracles occur when soul consciousness overrides self consciousness – when worldly cause and effect are overtaken by light and energy from the primal source of life. Turn away from what your mind has defined as suffering and you will face the ever-present, divine banquet of mercy and generous offerings. Face the world courageously and go through to its heavenly origin. Cut through space-time to the boundless and timeless and you experience the best of both worlds.

It is darkest before dawn. Anything which reaches its maximum limit will only turn to its opposite. Flow with life's rhythm and be carried away by god's will to the one essence and root of all creation.

5.2. PURSUING EXCELLENCE

The human desire for high performance, excellence, endurance or extreme action are examples of the self's yearning to go beyond normal boundaries. The soul is ever boundless and perfect and its shadow self aspires to that.

Every human intention or action is energised by the two powers of attraction and repulsion. Outer objectives change constantly with time but relate to the numerous desirable attributes and perfections, within the soul whose energy and frequency permeate our world. The need of the self to maintain peace and contentment are reflections of the actual state of the soul. All of the diverse divine qualities and attributes emanate from the soul's consciousness like the colours of a rainbow, each with a specific quality, frequency and wavelength. The meaning and purpose of life is to witness the ever-present perfections and harmony through the union of personal consciousness with soul consciousness.

Knowledge of perfection starts with self-awareness and the realisation of its dependency upon the soul and the perfect qualities therein.

The self is intrinsically attracted to the soul and its desirable qualities. The self seeks power because the soul knows limitless power. The self desires wealth whereas the soul is exposed to boundless treasures and wealth. The self loves longevity because the soul is eternal. Seeking outer pleasures are the childish attempts of the self to attain the state of the joyful soul. The mind is designed to capture and store worldly images and values, mirroring what the soul contains. Thus, all attempts by the mindful self to reproduce the soul's state are steps towards its ultimate surrender to the soul to achieve lasting contentment.

The self's desire for instant gratification is a flash reflection of the soul's natural state of contented joy. The soul is a beam of supreme consciousness, broadcasting its contentment. The self recognises this and tries to be like that.

The living universe is like a web of countless interactive fields and spheres of energies, following laws and principles at numerous levels. Physical, chemical, electro-magnetic forces, patterns, channels and programmes provide the diverse, intricate, unifying and interfacing relationships in existence.

This world is brilliantly designed to induce the seeker of knowledge to seek its source within higher consciousness.

These natural energy systems permeate and direct the flow of life's components along naturally evolving channels, producing specific entities or events with distinct vibrations and other characteristics. The primary cosmic source of creation energises and sustains all that is in existence according to intricate, inter-active designs and patterns, held together by the forces of attraction and repulsion, the inner and outer, meanings and form. The cauldron of this brew of life is the space-time sphere, which is miniaturised as the human mind, body, intellect and heart.

Romantics may talk about the glorious past. Some thinkers may express hope for a better future. The wise sage witnesses perfection at all times irrespective of the human condition.

The mind's nature is to confirm its own state by relating to other similar minds. In nature, an electrical charge is neutralized by its opposite and thus comes to rest; whereas the human mind desires to assert and confirm itself by similarities, until the mature self yields to its source and rests with its soul-mate. It is a natural human activity to wonder about the meaning and purpose of life on earth and to act in order to realise some desirable outcomes. If human consciousness was restricted to the space-time dimension only, we would have gone through life like animals without a quest or higher consciousness.

By experiencing change, awareness of everlasting truth emerges. To transcend the mind we must first know its limitations and function.

Human desires and needs never end. Thus, the self responds to numerous stimuli but acts according to what it considers important or attainable. Our desire for peace motivates us to perform actions which bring about harmony and tranquillity. The ever-present, perfect soul stimulates the self to strive for goodness and excellence at all times. This is an impossible goal to achieve for any length of time, because excellence relates to a situation and context, which are subject to change. Ultimately, the evolved self learns to admit its failure and surrenders to the soul's intrinsic perfections.

Desire to be free from all desires, then love perfection so passionately that you only witness the one perfect light behind all of creation's shadows.

The human desire for freedom and yearning for power and authority can be understood by studying the basic human make-up. We seek freedom not only from hunger and homelessness but also from ignorance, fear, uncertainty and other needs. Human poverty is both outer/material, as well as inner/spiritual. Outwardly rich people are often poor inwardly. The opposite is also sometimes true. Wholesomeness is the outcome of the balance between the outer and the inner. The self also desires authority, ability, knowledge and power at all times and continually quests for other divine qualities and attributes, until they are all found within the heart.

We desire freedom in order to exercise personal choices that lead ultimately to experiencing perfection. Real joy and thrill is the discovery of constant perfection, in spite of outer appearances and events.

The enlightened being is free from the illusion of independence or separation from the divine source of life and creations. By appropriately reading and following the map of creation, we shall experience numerous levels of knowledge and transformation. The enlightened being has no choice but to do the appropriate thing at the appropriate time and in the appropriate place. The more one knows the less are the personal choices, until one has no choice except an optimum one. This state is the outcome of unison between conditioned and pure consciousness.

Self-knowledge implies responsibility and knowledge of what to do or not, so as to be an agent and perpetrator of perfections.

The ultimate driving force of human life is the passionate desire and will to experience lasting goodness and perfection at all times. We yearn for the garden of Eden whilst drifting through a desert of confusion and loss. A diligent seeker is like someone in a boat rowing towards a hazy horizon, using the twin paddles of attraction and repulsion with the rudder of mental alertness as the navigational aide. The source of the power and energy behind attraction and repulsion is love of perfection. The successful boatman combines awareness of the boat, waves and weather conditions, whilst attuning an alert mind and inner intuition to the ultimate destination.

To live the present fully we need to be least concerned about the past and hopeful about the future and give in to the trusting, pure heart to lead us through the present.

As good and bad exist in every situation, it is a personal point of view that makes us select one or the other (or a mixture) of these values to judge the specific event, at any moment in time. Faults and shortcomings are reminders of missed perfections. Imperfections are incomplete perfections. The saying, 'ignorance is bliss', is the voice of darkness sounding as wisdom. All positive change or knowledge is a threat to this venomous self-assertive serpent. This is how the mind produces the ego and distracts the self from spiritual evolvement.

It is a wise person who is free from past limitations and uncertainties, hopeful about the future and lives fully with head and heart in the present.

For the evolving self, knowledge is the spiritual 'growth hormone' which will lead towards the garden of the heart. The spectrum of love for knowledge slides from zero (the basic childish mind), to some interest (the growing child), to preference (the motivated adult), to passionate pursuit (the committed seeker). It culminates in self knowledge and transformation by the unity of consciousness.

For worldly people, the more they gain wealth the more they desire it. For a spiritual seeker, the more one turns away from worldly pursuits the more one gains in heavenly insights and wisdom.

Pursuit of excellence is the key drive in life for it is fuelled by love of the perfect source behind creation. Excellence relates to both the process as well as the end, as it implies harmony and balance between the relevant opposites. Excellent food means suitability for the needs of the eater on multiple levels of culinary and nutritional aspiration. An excellent mind means clarity and accuracy in recall and reference to the intellect and relevance to the issue at hand. An excellent personal state implies a contented heart, irrespective of outer circumstances.

Everyone desires the best at all times, but as times change, so do desires and the definition of what is 'best'.

All orientations in the world point towards the perfect essence and source of known and unknown realities. All existence bears traces of the cosmic soul or god and reflects that aspect of the divine qualities. Wherever you look, there appears the face of god indicating his omnipresence.

The higher human state relates to inner knowledges and soul consciousness. Only then can one have true compassion, love and respect for the rest of creation.

The seeker is ever searching for ways to pierce the bubble of time and space to attain the state of boundless freedom. Only after submitting to this truth do we come to realise freedom by the direct experience of the supreme 'presence'. Unlike all worldly pursuits, the spiritual quest can only be achieved when all ambitions, desires and expectations are given up at heart. Asceticism, monasticism and puritanical tendencies are attempts to lessen personal desires and ambitions, thereby emulating the soul's perfect peace and contentment. Through voluntary and unconditional submission we transcend the mind and self consciousness, attaining the joys of self realisation.

How can you be content with only occasional pleasure when inner joy with its boundless bliss beckons you?

Worldly projects and challenges are necessary to develop the mind and intellect towards harmony between body, mind and heart. Most artistic or creative acts aim towards higher and subtler states of consciousness. The pursuit of well-being requires uniting the head and the heart in a state of optimum balance. Equally, excessive concern for physical or spiritual progress will detract from the natural ease and flow needed for awakening to that state of enlightenment.

Seek goodness and excellence in all your activities, irrespective of the outcome. What matters is constancy in intention, attention and attitude.

By recalling your past problems and fears you realise the fallacy and transience of what was considered important, urgent or distressing at that time. Essentially you are the same person now, although your self and mind have changed and grown. Your ability to refer to yourself as the same person is due to the constant soul within. The ever-changing personal consciousness is dependent upon this permanent reference point.

Always aim for excellence and perfection in every endeavour, whether it is a minor event or a major task. Act as though what you are doing is the most important action ever.

It is vital to combine a healthy, positive motivation with a flexible and cheerful disposition. With mental flexibility and a calm inner state the self will be in the best position to receive the appropriate guidance from head and heart. Human disdain for selfish opportunism comes from insight from the soul, reminding one to refrain from chasing shadows and being distracted from life's original essence. Selfishness is natural in childhood but in old age it is an ugly disposition. The soul is beyond selfishness or selflessness — it is pure mercy and grace. The self must learn selflessness and soulfulness.

Be patient with everyone, except with yourself, your lower tendencies and egotistical demands.

Whenever faced with failure, difficulty or constriction, look for the hidden opportunity, unexpected knowledge and insights within the situation. Do not simply label an event as a failure and miss witnessing the meanings and lessons therein. The truth lies beyond good and bad, beyond personal judgements and expectations are absent. Stress and concern are necessary conditions for appropriate change and evolvement in consciousness and knowledge. Equally, over-concern is a hindrance to growth. Human beings are naturally mentally stressed animals, seeking rest at heart.

Assume full responsibility for your conduct at all levels of body, mind and heart. Only then can you begin the process of diagnosis, analysis and re-evaluation from a fresh viewpoint.

Original love is the divine will and power for connecting and unifying all of existence. This primal divine love cascades into different levels bracketed between hate and passion. When love is directed towards someone or something, it becomes restricted and limited. This conditioned love can only lead to some disappointment. Love's essence is vast, limitless and unconditional. It is most excellent and perfect.

Unconditional love and passion shift worldly love and desires towards the sublime, heavenly, spiritual light and pure consciousness.

5.3. DESTINY AND FREEDOM

We desire freedom and choice in order to exercise our natural drive towards good outcomes and perfection.

The laws of nature follow their patterns and direction most efficiently. Human experience is the result of interacting with inner and outer events and situations. Personal destiny is the outcome of personal experiences that come about from taking a plunge amongst the waves and currents along the shore of life. We all desire to exercise our apparent 'free will' in order to reach that optimum mind/heart unison in intentions and actions.

Every being is the author of their own destiny, the experiencer as well as the witnesser, the actor and the audience.

The law of gravity will operate irrespective of who or what is being subjected to its force. Hence, an unfortunate personal destiny would be to have bones broken by a foolish jump from a high-rise building without means of cushioning the impact. Such an undesirable outcome can be avoided, however, by climbing down a rope or a ladder, rather than taking a free fall. Destiny can often change, as long as the self is flexible in taking references and accessing reason and rationality. Every moment is the destination of the previous one. Thus, a destiny is judged according to how the situation or event is perceived and evaluated by the person in relation to expectations.

Your destiny is the outcome of your inner state interacting with the outer world through mind and conditioned consciousness.

Although what is commonly meant by destiny is the future outcome of an activity or journey with no finality to anything until the end of one's worldly life. Even death is not final as far as the self and soul journey is concerned, although it demarcates a quantum change in consciousness and experience. Indeed, death can be described as an involuntary step towards perfection in the hereafter by discarding the physical body and space-time interplay.

With silence and inaction you still have the freedom of what to say or do; with speech and action you have, in that instant, surrendered your freedom.

Desires of the self are attempts to possess what the soul has. In reality, the soul is always content and complete in itself. The self desires to go beyond physical and mental limitations in seeking freedom from all boundaries — to fly, to disappear, to be rare, to have limitless powers, to be free and independent — in other words, to live as a soul.

The expression, 'larger than life', refers to boundlessness and the domain of the soul. Every self yearns for that state and can only attain it by surrendering to its soul-mate.

Personal destinies are linked with the outer world, with other people, the environment and other cultures and other factors. Group destiny will invariably affect an individual's destiny, and vice versa. One enlightened person at the right time in the right place can bring about major changes in the life of a society or nation, its quality of life and its future. This is where spiritually wise leadership is crucial in the growth of human consciousness and evolvement. Every day can bring new gifts of insights, knowledge and wisdom.

Success is commonly equated with worldly achievements. For the awakened self, success is the outcome of unity in consciousness.

Almost all sentient creatures in existence have a soul which broadcasts its coded messages in order to guide and lead the animal self to its proper destiny and fulfilment of its purpose. The ultimate intended destiny for human beings is the joy of the perfect moment and unity of consciousness. The changing outcomes experienced by the person depend upon the maturity and evolvement of the self and the extent of its reference to the soul.

The spiritual journey takes you past worldly changes and turmoil towards constant perfection, inner contentment and tranquillity.

Space is the canvas upon which time paints its colourful patterns. It is time that fills in space and renders the four customary dimensions of space-time into a grid of changing realities. The assumed consensus that time flows in one direction only is the result of collective habitual identification of the self with the growing body, mind and memories. There is no real logic or truth that the future is not before the present and that fulfilment did not precede the arousal of the need. Space-time is a confinement where energy fields interchange and exchange with countless entities being born and fading away. Particle physics, through its theories of reverse directions of time, black holes, unexpected probabilities and possibilities, interchange between matter and anti-matter and other strange occurrences, gives us an abstract picture that is not in line with the usual logic of human reasoning.

The quest of the self for freedom is its desire to be like the free soul in its boundlessness, independence, contentment and joy.

Paranormal phenomena, such as seeing past events or clairvoyance, are flashes and glimpses that soul consciousness transmits to the self. All experience is in space-time due to personal consciousness as energised by the soul, which in turn is the direct link with supreme consciousness or the cosmic soul. It is not, therefore, unusual for the evolved individual being to be able to foretell what is likely to work in the future and what is not. To be able to counsel with a gnostic or awakened being and follow their indicators is a great gift in life.

The heart connects this earthly world of body and mind with the heavenly domain of the soul.

When there is full connectedness between self and soul and unison between conditioned and pure consciousness, enlightenment is the result. This enables the person to witness perfection in the moment, whilst being aware of the background noises of worldly discord and apparent imperfection. The sage sees this life as a training ground and preparation for experiencing the eternal joys of the hereafter. The fool is sidetracked by short-lived pleasures and illusory worldly ambitions within the space-time confinement.

A fulfilled life is the result of the mature self following its intellect, spiritual intelligence and insights from the heart and higher consciousness.

Desire for freedom starts from outer physical limitations and progresses towards freedom at heart. We wish to control the outer environment and reduce dangers, fears and disturbances, so as to be free of needs in body, mind and heart. The self's desire to dominate and control echoes the soul's actual position of dominance and power. Real freedom only comes about as a consequence of the self's unconditional surrender to the soul. Real freedom liberates you from self-deception, misconceptions, veils and delusions. It delivers you to the eternal truth of your own soul. You can only be truly free from your lower self by being bonded with the higher.

The self fears what it doesn't know, thus it fears real freedom (subconsciously!) and openings beyond the mind, ego and sensations.

After freedom from material and physical needs comes the desire for freedom of mind, thought and expression; then freedom from all other desires except experiencing perfection at all times. It is the illusion of losing freedom that causes the self to avoid commitment or acceptance of responsibility. Freedom from outer or physical anxieties implies reliance on the inner, subtle guiding signs and indications from the heart. In that state the dividing line between the outer and inner domains disappear, as the outer and inner meet in harmony. Then the primal unity or gatheredness before creation and the apparent outer separation are reconciled. We seek freedom from limitations through outer movement and change, whilst the door to free happiness is through a trusting heart.

Inner freedom follows when the elusive desire for outer worldly or discernable freedoms is transcended. In truth bondage and freedom are never separate.

The quest for freedom follows a hierarchy from base needs for survival and growth to the ultimate spiritual fulfilment and inner freedom. To break the sound barrier the airplane shudders and needs a considerable boost in power. To go beyond the mind and ego barriers we also need an inner power to attain self transformation. True liberation will be experienced when the self realises it is totally dependent upon the soul, rather than chase outer independence and freedom. This is the call of religious pundits to depend upon God. Relative freedom is never totally satisfactory. Absolute freedom only comes with total surrender to pure consciousness and experiencing the perfection of the moment, which transcends all notions of freedom. When this harmonious convergence and unity between the different levels of consciousness occurs, time stops at that instant to reveal inexplicable perfection. This stillness in time is most sublime, as it reveals powerfully the divine presence of supreme consciousness.

Ultimate freedom has no structure, form or identifiable path to it. The key to it lies through self-surrender to the soul and its sublime root.

The concept of predestination often leads to fatalism and the denial of personal responsibility and choice. When a bumpy ride is experienced due to ignorance and lack of clear direction, we blame 'bad luck' or some other excuse, rather than admit personal responsibility. The self protects itself by blaming others for mistakes and misfortune. Another protection device is the idea of reincarnation. The origin of the term is *incarne*, 'within flesh', implying light within flesh, or the divine within the transient. Each soul is bound to its earthly agent or self and its journey towards the final abode of lights and essence. Every soul is like a fresh spark originating from the eternal divine light, whose purpose is to reveal the heavenly and earthly perfections for every person.

The self is always deceptive, seeking easy answers for everything whilst resisting the realisation of its own illusory subjective nature.

Personal destiny is experienced due to the interplay of numerous factors and forces, bringing about a final outcome. These powers and forces interact naturally in subtle, as well as discernable ways and in perfect order, even when we experience pain or suffering. In truth, there are only perfections seen or unseen, outer or inner, at all times; every moment bears the traces of perfect natural processes. At every level of existence there is a balancing act at play. A child who has experienced cruelty may want to become a policeman. An innocent youngster accused of wrongdoing may desire to become a judge.

Free will is a notion needed by the self to evolve to its potential union at heart with the soul, wherein there is no self image or concern for freedom, only unity.

The inexperienced self desires its independence and freedom, which, as we have seen, are the soul's qualities. The experienced and evolved self realises that its nature is a shadow companion to the soul: its duty is to totally align with and focus upon the soul, not upon its own egotistic image or mindset. Absolute slavery (to the higher) is akin to absolute freedom (from the lower). Emptying the self leads to fullness of the soul. Lasting fulfilment comes about when the self has surrendered to the soul and is in unison with it.

Real freedom is boundless, thus it is unknowable, for we only live within worldly bounds and know through limitations and relativities.

To witness the perfection of personal destiny, you need to 'step out of yourself' and look through the lens of the heart by the light of the soul's pure consciousness. Regarding a nation or society, you also need to step out of your relationship with that culture and its values before you can read accurately the state of a society and its well-being. To step *out* of the self requires stepping *into* the heart and the domain of higher consciousness. To hear or see *by* your heart you need to close your outer eyes and look *through* inner insight. This is when self consciousness becomes subordinated to soul consciousness.

The wise one is he who recognises outer discordance along with inner perfection, as seen through the eye of the soul.

6. WITNESSING PERFECTION

*As personal human consciousness evolves soul consciousness provides
the stable background behind the changes. When conditioned and pure
consciousness are unified, perfection is witnessed at all times.*

When the body is well and relaxed and the mind is still, a moment
of joyfulness may be experienced spontaneously without any
discernable reason. In such a state, time seems to stop or to move
smoothly. Concern for the future and sorrows of the past are
absent. When the heart is content, the self expresses a moment of
perfect harmony and peace. In such an instant personal
consciousness is synchronous with soul consciousness and the self
experiences harmony and the glow of profound well-being.

To witness perfection, all levels of consciousness need to relate
smoothly and harmoniously. If happiness and contentment is the
main purpose in life, then entry is through the door of experiencing and witnessing perfection always. The human desire for
outer success and excellence is only an aspect of aiming to realise
the perfect moment. We sometimes succeed in worldly activity
and at other times we fail. Pleasure through success is simply
reflecting the experience of momentary outer unity and harmony.
Even with failure, the events themselves have followed a perfect
pattern of cause and effect, irrespective of the final result and
personal feelings. There is, however, a danger that the spiritual
seeker may develop a cynical or careless attitude towards
outcomes. When someone expresses a lack of worldly interest and
claims that outer success does not really matter, the heart may still
harbour a secret desire or fear regarding pain or disappointment.
There is a big difference between hoping for something and acting
towards that end, and not hoping or acting yet having a hidden
fear or desire. Witnessing perfection at all times implies seeing the
outer and inner worlds with the soul's lens, not with the mind or

self. Action and outcome then do not matter as much from this transformative viewpoint.

6.1. REFLECTIONS OF PERFECTION

The purified heart reflects the light of the perfect soul or creator as it falls upon the receptive human self.

Everything in creation reflects, to a certain extent, an aspect of the numerous desirable qualities of the cosmic soul or god. These attributes are etched within the human soul and are sought after by the self. The lion is often thought to represent a symbol of power and dominance and the ant for selfless cooperation and collective survival. These attributes are universally regarded as virtues worthy to be pursued; and their absence or opposite qualities are vices to be avoided. All shadows are proof of the light which causes them. Every sentient creation has been touched by a spark of a perfect attribute of the universal essence through conditioned consciousness. Thus, everything in existence resonates with an aspect of the creator's perfections, or its opposite, at any one time.

Perfections are reflections of god's attributes. We experience aspects of them and also desire them. The soul contains these divine qualities and beams them out towards the self.

The self likes to be noticed and acknowledged when it is doing what is considered the right thing. It also wishes to hide its errors. Subconsciously the self knows of the higher qualities embedded within the soul and wishes to match them. This referencing is also called conscience. A mean person likes to be thought of as generous, a weak one as strong, an incompetent one as efficient. The self always aspires to the perfection of the soul. The self loves gifts, presents and good surprises: this reflects the nature of the soul, which is exposed to the divine treasury with its boundless gifts and generosity. The human appetite for 'freebies' or success with gambling or lotteries – rather than 'earning a living' – is the self's futile attempts to take on the soul's state of 'richness beyond needs'. Everything for the soul is free. The self loves new clothes, fashions or ideas. It also loves ancient objects or customs, for they invoke continuity, and timelessness – eternal qualities.. The soul is both timeless and ever-fresh (as it energises the self).

The soul is timeless but is here on earth with its companion body/mind self for a while, in order to bring back to gatheredness and unity matter and energy, as in body and soul.

The normal tendency for human beings is to appreciate a compliment, but excess flattery is rarely liked. Deep down the self is aware of its dark egotistical side and its falsehood. The self knows that there are always positive tendencies within it and that its nature is a composition of conditioned images. A wise person knows through the intellect that only the soul is worthy of praise. The self occasionally experiences the perfect presence; when the ego is at rest, the heart is content and the soul's light shines through. The obsession of the self for outer control in response to a world of constant change is distracting from unison with the ever present perfect order within the soul.

Give the self a chance to know itself and in time it will yield to its soul and come to rest at heart in contentment and bliss.

Everything in the universe is gradually expanding towards greater disorder ever since creation began (big bang) and departed from the point of 'perfect order'. Creation intrinsically starts as absolute order and then drifts into an apparent interplay between order and disorder. To experience a perfect true moment is to view the present through the timeless soul. This implies seeing only harmony irrespective of personal feelings or expecta-tions. To witness the perfection of the present implies freedom from emotions and personal judgments, fears and concerns of the future. The perfect moment transcends the notions of success and failure, space and time. While the seeker tries to experience perfection, the awakened person witnesses perfection in all events and situations — the exclamation, "Everything has turned out to be perfect!" becomes a constant observation.

Every situation contains an aspect of perfection; we need to find the right angle of vision and focus to see the entire scene through that aperture.

Humankind is at the pinnacle of creation in evolvement, consciousness and spiritual potential. As such we also carry a high responsibility towards other creations and life on earth. This state is referred to as man being god's agent, guardian or steward on earth. This responsibility is due to the privilege of being created in god's 'image', which is due to the human soul's exposure to the perfect divine attributes and qualities. As such we are all perfectionists at some time or another.

A truly free human being always witnesses perfection during the event. For others it is usually easier with hindsight. This state of awakening is accompanied by worldly and spiritual responsibility.

Love is the power which propels every self towards the soul along numerous steps of needs and desires. Initially we love and desire that which brings about contentment at physical, emotional and mental levels and peace at heart. Whenever you have an outer desire or need, remember that the soul within your heart has no needs. Restrict the desires of the self and remember the desireless soul. Ordinary people are motivated to acquire more wealth and power; the wise seeker desires access to the source of all wealth and power – the supreme source as evident within the heart.

The self is always driven towards the source of its inner life – the soul-mate within the heart.

Occasionally one experiences the elevated feeling of being at the centre of the universe. This happens when the self is in unison with the soul. With spiritual evolvement the self is lead by its passionate drive to unite with its soul-mate, which was always present but concealed behind space-time veils. The feeling of separation or loneliness drive the self towards illusionary outer gatheredness, worldly diversion and material security. Every self feels the pain and suffering of loneliness, inadequacy and incompleteness, until it surrenders to its soul. Then the spectrum of personal consciousness is immersed and fulfilled by the sublime supreme consciousness.

All drives and desires are outer responses to the divine caller, whose inner resident agent is the soul within the heart.

A spiritual seeker may be initially motivated by the love of paradise and fear of hell fire. The awakened person is no longer concerned about either, due to being absorbed in the love of the ever present perfection. Then comes passion, in which the lover has lost direction and identification, being lost in the beloved. In the outer world being lost is stupidity and ignorance, whereas in the inner world being lost to the essence is the entry into serendipity and bliss.

Every individual in this life strives at all times towards some perfection, whereas within the heart already resides the soul on the throne of the perfect kingdom of the microcosm.

Creation with its apparent diversity and complexities has originated from the primal state of perfect oneness. Every duality challenges us to discover the root of unity in them. The experience of outer dispersion and separation reminds the self to return to the state of original oneness. This is the reason why human beings like reunions and long to be with loved relatives and friends. The universal dispersion is held together by the unifying field and power of supreme consciousness, as it permeates the multitudenal strands and energy channels of creation. The mother's love for her baby is part of nature's programme for procreation, perpetuation and survival of the species and its evolvement. Conscientious parents show the child trust and reliability, so that the evolving self can grow to discover the ever trustworthy soul within the heart. Success in parenting is ultimately measured by the extent of delivering the child to its soul; the real divine parent or master.

Today's seed produces tomorrow's plant. Full attention to the present moment can lead to a more fulfilled future. Live fully the moment and you may glimpse eternal perfection.

We ask and wonder where we came from, why and what our destination is. Realism and pragmatism are all early steps of the self's journey towards higher consciousness. It is only through the evolvement of the self to the highest level of consciousness that it can relate outer events and situations with divine attributes and perfections and thus witness unity behind multiplicity. The puzzles and enigmas of life can never be resolved by intellect and reason alone. They can only dissolve in the spiritual light of a purified heart.

For the ordinary person a need is a problem to be overcome. For the reflective seeker a need is a reminder to call upon the generous god who is ready with its provision.

Human beings reflect the cosmic perfections at the point of conception but, as we grow errors and defects become prominent with increased entropy. Our apparent freedom of action only increases our imperfections. 'And time must have an end' is the ultimate and just remedy for all earthly endeavours. If we are willing to stop, our chances of an appropriate start are greater. When the stop/start frequency resonates within head and heart, the self and soul connection is stronger. Unity in consciousness is the fruit of spiritual evolvement which encompasses the seen and unseen worlds.

Maximum freedom in action also implies maximum possible mistakes and regrets.

Every event and situation contains within it perfection, but when the self is caught in the drama of the moment the opportunity to read the inner meaning of the event and its perfect root is often lost. As consciousness transcends the ego, however, and is focused exclusively upon the present moment, insight reveals a new dimension of truth. When one reads through the soul's lens one will discover deeper meaning and knowledge. When the mirror of the self faces the soul, it will reflect its perfection. To give meaning and purpose to life does not mean you will not have outer desires and varied worldly projects. What it means is that your worldly activities are aligned with the deeper goal and hope of reaching the state of inner contentment, and peace at heart.

Listen to the message behind what you see and you will discover amazing harmony. Behind every specific consciousness there is higher consciousness. Unite both.

Permanent divine perfection is the essence of what appears as imperfect. The light of truth cascades down to all of creation at numerous levels of clarity. God's light is permanent and eternal. It is the source of all existential lights and shadows. Layers and levels of divine perfections encompass all of existence. It is according to one's spiritual evolvement and purity at heart that one can witness this truth. The ultimate state a seeker aspires for is to complement outer sight and sound with insight and meaning of sound

Divine justice is in operation at all times but often we are veiled from seeing how subtle and pervasive it is. Until we exercise fairness and justice on earth, we will continue to suffer aggression and warfare — that is part of divine justice, for it encompasses human justice as well (short-lived) injustice.

6.2. SELF-REALISATION

Enlightenment is the result of unison between self and soul – alignment at all levels of consciousness. When the soul rules supreme peace and contentment prevail over the human kingdom.

The self draws its life from the soul, which in turn beams its energy of consciousness through the body, mind and senses. The self, then, evolves through maintaining balance and equilibrium between the inner (mind, senses etc.) and the outer worlds. Further maturity, growth and wisdom takes place through refinement of intentions and actions and clearer links between head and heart. Spiritual awakening begins to be enjoyed and to be more and more a way of life.

The intuitive centre is your heart and is closer than you imagine. Still outer noise and you will hear the silent inner voice.

Personal consciousness is derived from soul consciousness. This inherent dependency drives the self restlessly to seek its security and self sufficiency. However, whatever the person achieves in this world will not satisfy the thirst for the permanent other-worldliness. The self resorts to all kinds of tricks, including drugs and intoxicants, in the hope of releasing it from its impossible intrusive addiction. We love power and control, yet we also enjoy moments of deliberate loss of control, such as when diving or paragliding. The self always seeks the boundless freedom and power of the soul. The individual's experience of expansion in mind, knowledge and connections, propels it towards the bound-lessness of the starting point with its vast possibilities.

Self-knowledge begins by turning away from egotistical mental shadows towards the soul's contented and durable state, where the root of all knowledge lies.

Self-realisation is the state of spontaneous and synchronous awareness of the self, mind, heart and all inner and outer landscapes, courtesy of the soul. The extent of the efficient response to the outer world indicates the level of the evolved self and its maturity. All human beings are self-serving. The question is: which aspect of the self is being served or addressed? There are countless levels and lenses of the human self. There is the enclosed egotistical childish self; there are numerous blaming selves; there are countless inspired selves. As one grows, the mind can provide numerous sets of lenses and interpretations of the inner and outer worlds.

The less the self is concerned with worldly matters, the greater the soul's receptivity to messages and guidance via the heart.

People who excel in the material world are unlikely to be able to give sufficient attention to the exploration of the inner subtler realms. Love, trust and absorption in the outer world may harden the heart and hinder spiritual progress. Worldly people are often given a chance to reflect upon meanings and higher purposes through failures and difficulties, but their persistent mental habits and egos block inner openings and a balanced life.

The wise and illumined person has a strong sense of right and wrong, deep interpersonal ties, a friendly disposition, clear ethics, awareness of boundaries and responsibilities, a healthy sense of humour, creativity, originality, compassion and understanding of people's limitations and needs. The wise seeker, with commitment and trust in the perfection of the moment, accepts with understanding every situation as factual, deals with it ratio-nally, efficiently and with a cool head and warm heart. Initially, one looks for outer references and guidance, until the inner soul reference shows the way. Then human logic and rationality will connect with divine justice and will.

The seeker is looking for the light of truth; the enlightened being sees by the light of truth. One is searching for light, the other lives by it.

There are two main types of euphoria. One is the eureka of a special discovery, breakthrough and insight, which brings about discernable delight and joy. Such insights occur when conditioned consciousness goes beyond thought into the creative vistas of pure consciousness. The other type of euphoria is deep, calm and without outer excitement. It relates to the permanent presence of supreme consciousness. This transcendental state reveals self awakening and spiritual maturity: when thoughts cease and shadows disappear, one is engulfed in the oceans of lights and luminous delights.

Trust in truth and you will experience it, for it has been with you always but veiled by biology and other tissues and issues. The divine light forever shines but the inner eye is usually closed.

The enlightened person always experiences win-win situations at heart because of witnessing perfection at all times. Outwardly, the self acknowledges the win-lose, as well as lose-lose situations. At all times the soul resides regally and utterly contentedly within the heart. Those who have not fully accessed the state of enlightenment are always caught in win-lose situations and the challenges of inner/outer battles. Yet everyone aspires for constant success: an outer impossibility but a desirable inner possibility.

The awakened self hears the clear inner voice. Other selves battle with confusion (outer noises) and conflict before arriving at the safety of the knowing heart.

When the serious seeker experiences ease, he is grateful. When he experiences difficulty, he is patient, understanding the limitations of circumstances. Inherited outer human disadvantages, such as genetic handicaps (e.g. physical shape or size) will fade away in comparison to the potential wonderment of self realisation and inner contentment. The sage's inner and outer state is at ease, as he sees the goodness in everything. Every self is seeking to worship at the altar of the heart, it longs for the soul and its abode of perfection. The awakened self has already surrendered to its soul and its master. When the gold prospector discovers King Solomon's inexhaustible mines, he will abandon further search. The same is true when you find god's light within the soul. When you reach the shore of supreme consciousness all other levels of awareness fade away.

The self will experience expansion, openings and delight when it realises the boundless generosity, grace and mercy of god and divine qualities within the soul.

Self-knowledge brings about inner stability due to the unification of the two domains of consciousness: personal and pure consciousness. The self was caught within space-time and had to climb out of the confused world of relativity back to the realm of the soul beyond space-time. The eternal soul was always there to energise and beacon its companion self. There is no end to levels of self-knowledge and enlightenment, until the light of oneness shines through all dualities and cements the unison between self and soul and establishes unity in consciousness as it had at the inception of creation.

Enlightenment is to witness perfection within every situation.

The wise sage regards this world as presenting examples and paradigms of what exists in the unseen world and the hereafter.

Enlightenment is not a natural or guaranteed outcome of struggle against the lower self and ego. Self awareness and spiritual discipline simply reduce waywardness, worldly distractions and sufferings. Enlightenment is a divine gift, which arrives when the seeker is ready and able to accept its might and bewildering power. Enlightenment resolves the intrinsic difference between change and constancy, what is limited and earthly, or what is boundless and heavenly, by dissolving all space-time barriers. Soul and self merge in the heart of the awakened being. The self is like an identifiable photon, which needs to recognise that the soul is the source of both particle and wave. The evolved self sees itself alternating as both photon and wave, thereby uniting conditioned and pure consciousness.

Enlightenment is the art of lifting the self from its specific identity to be engulfed by the ever present and eternal ocean of unity and supreme consciousness.

The disciple declared that there are countless beings in existence, but the master insisted that there is none except one. He then reminded the student that when you truly open your eyes many may appear within your sight, whereas in truth these are only shadows of the everlasting one light within them, before them and after them. The master then sang: 'Passion for god has bewildered me; thus I am alien and a stranger in this world. When I appear he (god) vanishes, and when he appears I vanish.'

The enlightened being acknowledges the self's needs and its dependency upon the soul. He is in unison with the supreme consciousness, which gives sentiency to self and soul. The enlightened being never denies this world but always sees and acknowledges the supremacy of the one essence within all worlds, tangible or unseen.

6.3. LIVING BY GRACE

When you exercise mercy and compassion upon earthly creation, the heavens shower greater gifts upon you. When you allow goodness to flow through you, divine grace overflows.

When the supreme consciousness rules over self consciousness, divine grace and presence overflows from the heart. Then every moment is experienced and witnessed as perfect, irrespective of the outer events, personal views or opinions. The first steps toward this destination include understanding of cause and effect and the subtler connections between the two. It is much easier to witness perfect relationships and connectedness in nature, such as in insect or bird life. It is more difficult to witness perfection when there is personal or emotional involvement. Such self concern, fear of the future, past habits and preoccupation with thoughts and other distractions divert one from experiencing the sublime moment. Perfection was at the inception of creation. It has always been there but was subtly veiled by the sense and mind (the imaginal sense) awaiting discovery. Flashes of insight usually occur during deep meditation and often when least expected.

Letting go of what is not yours (everything) is the necessary step to letting in that which is yours (the soul) – the carrier of the essence of everything.

Freedom, success, happiness and all other desirable ideas or situations are energy patterns already present both in the outer world, as well as in the inner heart. The human struggle is the attempt to unify outer awareness (experience) of this 'rainbow' with the inner (pattern) presence within the soul. All of these qualities become discernable when the self is focused towards non-forms, inner meanings and soul consciousness. Prayers, meditation and other spiritual practises take the self out of the 'hard-wired' region of mind and reason and onto the hazy land of the subtle domain of energy patterns and spiritual 'lay-lines'.

In this world, desires never cease. In the hereafter, they cannot be acted upon. Humankind is the bridge between the restless self (earthly) and the contented soul (heavenly).

With the realisation of life's great potential, every moment becomes precious and is given its due respect and importance. To be deliberately enslaved to the supreme cosmic light is to be free from other shadows. It is by god's generosity, mercy and grace that we turn away from our egotistical dark shadows towards the luminous light of the soul within the heart. Prophets, messengers and enlightened beings have awakened to this companions and guides along the spiritual path. These revealed knowledges cannot be reached by reason, wisdom or supplication. They need to be imbibed or absorbed through passion.

Celebrating presence implies an end to absence. The eternal is ever present. Awareness of it occurs when outer and inner consciousness unify.

The prophetic make-up is so refined and attuned to supreme consciousness that the high voltage and power of this cosmic light is in constant unison with the prophetic personal consciousness. As such, all prophetic knowledges and actions directly reflect divine light and will. When prophetically revealed lights reach their full maturity and completion the overflow nourishes the rest of creation.

To trust and love the prophetic being is to love one's own perfect soul.

Living by god's grace is to transcend the illusion of the self's independence, its own will, ability, knowledge and source of power. To realise god's light within the soul does not release the self from watchfulness against the dangers of self-indulgence and the pitfalls of the ego. Living by grace does not imply denying outer forms but seeing earth as a stepping stone to the heavens and even a part of it. Enjoying the full moon and its cool light enhances the appreciation for the qualities of the effulgent sun. They complement each other as they perpetually relate to each other.

Love and care of the self and its kingdom of body, mind and heart is a prelude to the understanding of god's kingdoms on earth and in the heavens.

God's mercy and grace permeate the fabric all of existence. Everyone yearns to trust and realise ever-present divine perfection. Yet, most people prefer the temporary shelter of what we (outwardly) already know and lack the courage to plunge into what is new or strange. Hence prophets are denied by their own people; so are other enlightened beings. Freedom from worldly confusion can only occur when the self is submerged in the soul's energy fields of higher consciousness. It is revealed that no human being ever enters the garden by actions alone, although without appropriate selfless action the ego would dominate and lead the self into deeper ignorance, despair and confusion. Before reaching the garden we need to get out of hell. God's grace encompasses every situation, desirable or otherwise. By seeing the perfection of the moment, you will be guided to appropriate action or inaction. You will thus respond aptly to the situation rather than react emotionally or irrationally.

Coalesce your desires into one supreme one: to be desireless. Do not fear creation and do not be anxious about your provisions.

By selfless good actions the self turns away from the ego and the other veils and distractions. It begins to discover soul consciousness and divine proximity and presence. The self experiences relief when it realises that all power and control reside within the soul and that all along it was a mere shadow pretending to have independence and freedom. We emerge from the dark womb of ignorance challenged by love of excellence until we reach the uplifting vistas of perfect divine presence.

Self-reliance is ultimately soul dependence and god acceptance.

Each soul is like a spark from the cosmic divine light, thus it contains all its qualities. Each spark then drifts into the space-time world and takes on distinct characteristics and personality through the self, body, mind and other appendages. The self or personality veils the soul with the body, mind, senses and other earthly qualities. The mind and memory give value to worldly experiences and generate personal expectations, prejudices, hopes and fears, as the self grows and evolves towards fulfilling its destiny.

Do not wait to stumble on the perfect moment. Look for aspects of inner perfection in every moment. Do not ignore all if you can't attain it all.

When the self is exposed to the vistas of the heart through soul consciousness, the value of its previous attachments and priorities changes. For the journey of self-knowledge to begin the heart needs to be kept pure for the light of the soul to shine through. The weaknesses of the heart are numerous, mostly due to negative tendencies and adverse behaviour, such as self-indulgence, extravagance, meanness, cowardice, arrogance, pettiness, apathy, despair, cunning, enmity, dishonesty and the numerous other vices of the egotistical self. It is for this reason that most spiritual paths and religions advocate righteous actions and an ethical and virtuous way of life, based on selfless service to others in order to clear the heart and purify it.

Lasting relief, durable contentment and freedom from insecurity come about when the self submits to the grace and mercy of divine presence within the purified heart.

Every self desires the attributes and perfections of the soul; the self draws nourishment and hope from them. Once the self yields, submits and gives in to its soul then a unified and stable condition of being 'centred,' 'present,' and authentic is attained; normal neuroses vanish and deep cheerfulness prevails. Total madness is very close to total sanity. Madness occurs when the psyche is fragmented and the self loses sight of the soul. Total sanity is the self losing itself in the boundless domain of the soul and pure consciousness.

The perpetual human drive for idealism and perfection are reflections of the self searching for its perfect soul-mate.

The journey of the self begins in the company of an ego and ends in the embrace of the soul within the inner heart. The ego to the self is like the dry outer shell of a seed to the kernel: the water of consciousness (or living conscience) through knowledge and correct action will crack the outer shell, allowing the self to grow to know the soul, yielding the fruit of gnosis.

The more the self is free from the ego and its countless veils, the more one can be attuned to the wholesome inner soul.

Every moment contains an aspect of the past as well as the future. Yet, every fresh moment is free of past and future. When personal consciousness merges fully with soul consciousness, it experiences bliss and happiness. Much personal discipline, accountability and other spiritual efforts are needed to reach the abode of perfect presence, which is ultimately due to divine grace. Pursuit of disciplined knowledge and wisdom are necessary for grooming the self but can themselves become serious obstacles in final transformation if they become new spiritual 'status'. The self must give up everything, including love of wisdom and spirituality. The conscious search for enlightenment is a good starting point but this desire must be forgotten along the journey of this divine love affair. Absence of all desires is what takes the seeker to the threshold of enlightenment where there is neither seeker nor sought, just the ONE beyond description.

When you unconditionally and sincerely give up all you begin to realise the presence of the essence of all.

Some ancient cultures described and experienced every creation as a manifestation of god. Some Bushmen frequently practiced trance ceremonies and 'out of mind' experiences. Such transcendental and visionary events were recorded on cave walls and passed on as part of folklore and later as 'art'. On occasion, the leading shaman might take on the personality of the eland, which, in its flight, bursts its liver and bleeds to death, thus moving on to the other world. The voluntary death of the self often signified the resurrection of the soul to the 'beyond' country of timelessness. Several African churches incorporate aspects of ancient spiritual possession and other customs of 'charisma', 'spirit communications' and other forms of 'mindlessness' in their practises. Civilised countries increasingly miss the simple joy of accessing soul consciousness. Drugs and alcohol are poor substitutes and come with heavy penalties for health, economy and quality of life.

Enlightenment results when the self loses its 'separate' identity and differentiated consciousness and unites with supreme consciousness.

Human history is a slow progress report on the evolution of human biology as well as consciousness, where mistakes and distractions are highlighted and dramatised by 'extinctions'. Whenever there has been growth in knowledge and higher quality of life, commentators have labelled those periods as 'ages of enlightenment' or 'golden years'. There have been many such stages in human history. However, due to the natural tendency of the self to be indulgent, lazy and egotistic, human beings have expected quick solutions and salvation from religious charlatans, heroes, miracle workers, charismatic leaders, tyrants, despots, or anyone who promises instant victory and happiness. To serve or help humanity in a genuine and durable way, a leader needs to help people help themselves responsibly, with accountability and transparency at every level. This path is time consuming and doesn't appeal to a quick result mentality.

An evolved being shuns power and influence over other beings for he/ she is aspiring to know the source of universal power and consciousness, which is the essence of all powers.

The appropriate way ahead for humankind is balanced inter-action between head and heart, rationality, spiritual insight and personal and societal accountability. First consult the mind, then refer to the heart, then act according to the least selfish option even though it may be difficult. Serve others and discover that, in truth, you are only serving your higher self. Compassion is sympathy with understanding and responsive action with love. Unconditional compassion is beyond love and hate. It is pure overflow of generosity. Spiritual progress requires the self to admit ignorance and be in submission and humility. Desire for religious rank or other spiritual positions or status is a major obstacle in the path of truth. Be cautious about your sub-conscious!

Acknowledge and respect all creation, then transcend it all to the majesty, beauty and the power of the present moment and witness its perfection.

Well-being of body, mind and heart are essential for spiritual growth and unison betweens self and soul. The body is like a temple: for an aspiring worshipper, its health and efficiency are important. The danger comes from being infatuated with a beautiful temple rather than the pervading divine beauty. As for the seasoned seeker, the entire earth is a temple. Thus, a holistic life for individuals, as well as for society, implies outer health in order to pursue inner health and harmony and contentment. Commitment to a path and appropriate spiritual practices are essential if the self is to unite with its soul-mate and bask in god's eternal grace and mercy. Worship initially satisfies the need to attempt an escape from undesirable situations, mindsets or behaviour. Then worship becomes the mode of life, as it brings the person closer to witnessing perfection. To live by grace and divine presence is to be in awe at all times and in the grip of the miraculous divine light with its visible manifestations and boundless domains.

It is only the wise who are constantly awed by the realisation of how immensely sublime every situation is, how glorious every moment is, how shattering god's light presence is. Thank god for all the veils and barriers!

7. RESPONDING TO SIGNS: SUMMARY

The universe is alive and responsive at multiple levels of energy, consciousness perception and subtler links. The evolved human self interacts and relates at different levels with the mind, senses, intellect and heart and soul.

The interactive universe maintains its overall equilibrium by natural exchanges between matter, energy and numerous other forces at different levels and degrees of magnitudes. This multidimensional cosmology contains countless realities and entities that attract and repel each other, which are created and destroyed with varying life spans. The human position in creation is unique for it embraces all the physical and material aspects in existence, as well as a metaphysical dimension that is unseen, intangible, essential and most influential. The natural physical laws are the first to attract human attention and investigation by the mind and senses. The metaphysical and spiritual domain, however, is elusive and does not fit within the worldly patterns of logic and causal or mathematical elegance.

This chapter highlights aspects of the inner or hidden dimension in creation and draws some patterns, descriptions, 'spiritual logic' and precepts, which may be helpful for the seeker as a pocket atlas. The root of this viewpoint is the islamic prophetically revealed knowledge in the Qur'an and the messenger's teachings, as applied and lived by numerous – famous, as well as less recognised – spiritual masters, imams, sufi shaykhs and other enlightened beings. To apply this teaching effectively in a transformative mode, we need to be sensitive to the signs and signals from head and heart and from close and far horizons. When we read and apply these maps sincerely, faithfully and confidently, step-by-step, with cautious and responsible awareness, the outcome is without doubt astonishing evolvement and awakening to a transformed life.

The awakened heart is conscious of the complex interplay of the opposites and especially that of energy and matter, all of which is sustained by a unifying root and cosmic essence.

7.1. THE SENTIENT MAP

The human body is like a mobile home for the self: restless to explore and travel wider afield. Without an interactive map, however, the driver will become confused, frustrated and disheartened.

Human life combines two distinct domains of consciousness: the personal domain of the self, as experienced by the senses and physical descriptions; and the subtle, pure consciousness of heart and soul. These two powers meet, interact and complement each other to varying degrees of synchronicity, whilst maintaining their respective integrity. Windows of creativity and insights open during periods when the self is relaxed, not over concerned with the outer world. As for worldly creations, everything that is discerned by us is subject to duality and complementary opposites, the root of which is the ever prevailing cosmic unity.

To read the situation accurately, the self must be flexible, the mind clear and adaptable, the heart pure, open and illumined.

The serious traveller in this world needs to read and understand the meaning of the numerous dimensions and levels of the map, decode them and act appropriately to avoid pitfalls, in order to arrive safely at the desired destination. Travelling along the middle path means being balanced between the earthly space-time realm and heavenly boundlessness. These two domains meet in the heart of an evolved being, at the threshold of high consciousness.

Act with sincerity and responsibility without over concern about the outcome. Your inner state must be steady and centred during progress, as well as at arrival.

The idea of evolution, according to natural selection, is challenging because it implies the presence of an innate design, leading to perfection at numerous levels. A few million years ago, the size and strength of an animal indicated superiority and perfection. Then versatility and adaptability redefined power, strength and survival skills. Then came higher intelligence with the result that whatever entity is endowed with greatest intelligence is most fit to endure and evolved. Intelligence is an aspect of consciousness which is the essence and power behind creation and its evolvement. Ultimate evolvement is when self awareness (conditioned consciousness) is in alignment with supreme consciousness.

Life on earth has evolved from a most humble beginning and human life reproduces all aspects of creations, low and high.

The quality of human life is a function of the self's responses to a whole range of stimuli: physical, mental and spiritual, from within and without. We constantly strive for equilibrium and balance at numerous levels of consciousness. For success in the material world, we need to evaluate and investigate causal and factual conditions, analyse and plan before any action is undertaken. It is always one's personal state and viewpoint that gives the value of acceptance or rejection to any situation. Quality and quantity and one's idea of good or bad are relative and relate to proportionality and attempts to restore balance and harmony between mind, heart and the outside world.

Past experiences are useful references to understand the present. More important, though, is the voice of the pure heart.

Human growth, physical maturity, mental discipline, intellect, creativity and higher developments are all road markers towards the balanced state of harmony within the spectrum of consciousness and alignment between self and soul. Constant awareness, at all levels, is needed to maintain an optimum state. Then the invisible patterns of the fabric of creation will reveal meaningful designs and landmarks, which, if read and followed will lead to desirable conclusions. When desire and hope are connected, a healthy and positive drive may lead towards an understandable and perhaps acceptable end. When desire is not backed by hope or action, frustration or anger may be the outcome.

Everything in existence announces its real meaning and purpose through sound, sight and other means of communication and language.

To develop and exercise a rational mind requires systematic discipline, according to worldly logic and wisdom. Anarchy is a human attempt to reproduce natural chaos without its intrinsic order, its boundaries and its special (hidden or different) logic. To open the vistas of the heart, however, one must turn away from all thoughts and tangible discernments towards higher consciousness. The mind is the king of the earthly body while the heart is the throne of the soul, representing heavenly rule. To know the heavens we must leave earthly rules and connect with the soul and read its scripture. A person's body may not seem perfect but the root of all perfection lies within the soul. It is up to us to discover and live it according to that design. Heaven on earth is a metaphor for soul within the heart in a body.

The self is restless and will not give up its natural waywardness or accept boundaries unless it is given a better incentive and more joyful alternative pursuit.

Most human beings experience varied distractions and difficulties in the pursuit of spiritual knowledge. The dynamics of self, heart and soul need to be properly understood and the appropriate signs read and followed. The self tends to postpone higher calls, whereas lower (physical or mental) desires always take precedence. It is absurd logic to think if a little of something is good for us, then a lot (of the same) is better. Equally that if much of something is bad, then a little of it also will be bad. A little fear of uncertainty is always good, whereas too much of anything is always bad.

Emotions often confuse and distort factual events and information. The seeker on a clear path needs to follow the direction given by intellect, heart and soul.

The human soul reflects the universal soul and draws from the supreme consciousness its soul consciousness. This light is then caught as personal consciousness when it experiences body, mind, senses, events and other situations. The soul is infused by divine love, mercy, knowledge (and other qualities), whilst the feeble self, which is the earthly shadow of the soul, constantly desires to be loved and acknowledged. People desire to be loved for 'who they are', for their own sake, not for wealth, looks or usefulness. This is only meaningful if 'their own sake' means their innermost soul, rather than the changing self or ego. The self experiences both acceptance as well as rejection during its restless pursuit of the elusive security and constant tranquillity and bliss.

The soul/self partnership is like that between the (hidden) root and (visible) trunk of a tree: they are totally interdependent. The self acts in the visible world of branches and leaves and responds to changing seasons, whilst the soul silently and invisibly provides constant nourishment.

The difference between thinking through the mind and listening to the heart is that the mind refers to past experiences, images and values, as well as future concerns, whereas the heart refers to truth, which is timeless. The rational mind acts relatively and is subject to change whenever it is wise to do so, whereas the heart reflects unchangeable truth. Emotions are mental shadows caught in the cul-de-sac of the mind, which leave their impact psychologically as well as physically. Reliable guidance is the result of heavenly light cast upon the dark earth. It is the inner meaning which gives purpose to outer form; it is the heart that leads the self to its ultimate purpose, which is union with the soul.

The desire for independence in this world and the human love for self-reliance and independence are reflections of the qualities of the soul upon its shadow, the self.

If the self is to remain in balance it needs to be aligned at all times with the soul. It is natural for the self to be restless in its elusive search for freedom. Yet, the self also longs for continuity and constancy, which is the intrinsic nature of the soul. The immature self loves to be the centre of attention and acknowledgment and it resents seeing others in that position. Jealousy is the self's childish desire for exclusivity. The self desires the state of the soul, which is always god's favourite.

A fragmented, insecure and volatile person broadcasts the need for rehabilitation and equilibrium. This healing can occur best through self-awareness and responsibility for all intentions, thoughts and actions.

The human self is always curious and interested in viewing other people's grief and afflictions. This human emotion often leads to empathy or sympathy which is an expansion of consciousness. The childish self during a moment of pain puts up a brave face, yet it also exaggerates pain to draw attention when the image of bravery is lost. The human love of solving puzzles or solving a mystery is a small reflection of the inborn desire to discover the mysterious soul within. We love to keep a secret, yet we desire to discover or expose secrecy. The ultimate secret is the soul, its perfect qualities and timelessness. We love some surprises and dislike others. A surprise is loved when it expands the self and is hated when it restricts the self. In truth, whatever leads the self to yield to its soul is a good move, irrespective of whether it is considered a good or bad surprise.

The soul contains all possible patterns and designs of creation while the self desires to discover them in tangible form, reflecting what is within the soul in the outer world.

Detailed specific prescriptions and remedies for the seeker on the path differ according to the overall situation and inner state of the seeker. Context, relevance and priorities are key for any progress. Personal responsibility, disciplined accountability and wise counsel are essential at all times. Confusing emotions and distorted personal visions are due to egotistical bias and mental limitations. Speed up time by a hundred years and then look back at your present desires. Add fifty years of age to your beloved partner or companion and then consider your attitude. Still your mind, empty your heart and dive into the infinite moment. Then you are closer to spiritual awakening.

There are evolved beings with much earthly wisdom; learn from them the ways of the world. There are fewer people with spiritual wisdom and light; learn from them the ways of the heavens. Then there are the few who have absorbed earthly and heavenly lights; let your heart be exposed to them and hope to resonate with their state. Absorb their enlightened silence.

The human mind and memory are always in danger of distracting the self from its principal purpose of evolving towards the domain of the heart and soul. The company one keeps has a much greater influence upon one's inner state than we realise. Being

with people whose main concern is worldly pleasure and acquisition will undoubtedly tarnish the heart of the seeker proceeding
along the path of abstention. Strength and skill in one domain are
often a sign of weakness in the other. Worldly wisdom without a
heavenly reference and accountability is mainly a clever manipu-
lation of others and will ultimately lead to (inner) disappointment.

Desire and greed increase with success in worldly matters, including the
quest for (outer) knowledge, just as thirst increases when one drinks
salty water.

It is not possible to love and respect this world and not be afflicted
by it. A bird desiring to eat the fruit of a tree that is kept under a
net does so at its own peril, as the net will ensnare it. To act in this
world while referring to the soul and divine purpose is to act with
awareness and presence of a rational mind and a purified heart,
without any anxiety about the future or regrets for the past. A
wise person does not deny the changing world and all its relative
experiences and values, but maintains a constant reference to the
absolute, eternal and ever-present truth. A normal adult generally
likes to appear assertive and confident. An evolved person is
tolerant, compassionate and easy-going. An enlightened person
sees through the eye of 'truth' and is sometimes perceived as soft,
at other times difficult and hard. It is difficult for a novice to be in
close proximity to an enlightened being. The two radar screens
don't show similar readings.

Your understanding and dealings with the changing outer world whilst
aware of the inner truth behind outer events is a good sign of your
spiritual evolvement.

The duality in the composition of human nature and the interplay
between self and soul is like a transparency which, when placed on

any human situation, will bring to light the essential components and will resolve most issues considered difficult or confusing. All human behaviour follows patterns to do with the self in a specific context but ultimately with reference to the highest values or virtues, which lie within the soul. This map of truth can be read accurately and applied in the relative world of change and divergence when the self is least veiled by the prejudices of the mind, ego and emotional concerns. When outer sight and inner insight are in unison then the moment yields its true nature. Uncertainty and confusion will yield to clarity and contentment.

The self will find ease and harmony if it follows the pattern inscribed within the soul. By growing and evolving with the natural cycle of seasons both outwardly and inwardly, the self will arrive at paradise with its perpetually perfect season.

If you embark upon this journey you will experience what lies behind the scenery and arrive at the inner source of blissful contentment. As this journey is a spiritual pilgrimage, you will personally experience the true adventures and thrills that lie beyond maps and directions. This is the world of insight, inspirations, meanings and gnosis of the invisible world within and beyond. To qualify for this undertaking, one needs utter humility, bereftness of the self and total dedication to truth. It takes courage to go beyond the mind, self-images and all other human concerns. To experience eternal 'ongoingness' one must not only go beyond the natural barrier of the ego, sense, intellect and reason, but also past 'death'. Eternal light has always been the nature of the soul but the self experiences life within the confines of space-time. Unity of self and soul marks a beginning with no end

Internalised information will bring about transformation and unity in consciousness.

7.2. LIVING THE MAP

The most genuine and authentic human need is to align the self with its soul. Most outer desires distract the self from its goal.

After reading the map of creation and understanding its codes the wise traveller integrates the inner and outer readings with the context, so as to maintain an optimum state, while moving along the highway of consciousness. With practice and experience, reinforced by correcting mistakes, living the map becomes a natural and enjoyable journey. Reading the situation correctly, then interacting with all its elements, is the first step along the path of transformation and accessing to higher consciousness. When this holistic state of inner and outer referencing becomes established, there will emerge, over time, the integrated and authentic person guided by intellect and spontaneous intuition.

To maintain the correct direction towards your destination, you need to listen to your heart and respond faithfully.

The 'middle way' or 'straight path' does not imply mediocrity or lack of thrill; it is exposure to the full spectrum of all realities. If you are on the edge of a path, you will only see the part nearest you but when you are in the middle you have a better view of both extreme sides of the pathway. The human journey needs to be guided by the mind and senses, as well as the heart and soul. The middle path is at the centre of these gridlines.

Remain outwardly ordinary, whilst discovering the extraordinary inner dimensions of life. Pay attention to the road but keep your ultimate focus upon your destination.

Every body, mind and emotion is subject to the relative world of time and space with its specific dimensions and limitations. We consider our world as real and desire stability and predictability in it, yet the so-called material foundations of our world are based on an amorphous and illusory subatomic domain, with most of its entities being grey matter, black holes, plasma, non-discernable or intangible sub-particles. The laws of logic of quantum physics are dramatically different from the world of classical physics. The same parallel duality applies with regard to human consciousness and life. The conditioned personal consciousness is like our outer world, whereas soul consciousness is another entity and not subject to the space-time limitations. The same way that the outer natural world is balanced by an inner world of particle physics, human consciousness is founded upon soul consciousness and its root of supreme consciousness.

The observable world is finite, alluding to infinity.

The rise of consciousness begins at babyhood, instigated by sensing movement and change. This basic and crude awareness grows and evolves along several dimensions through input from the senses and mind. The adult experiences the outer and inner senses, memories, emotions and numerous other stimuli almost simultaneously. This is what distinguishes human beings from other evolved primates. The uniqueness of human consciousness is its ability to experience its conditioned awareness, as well as higher consciousness, which transcends space-time. The animal self is primitively coupled with its body and mind. When a bird is captured, it is as though it has died. It has only conditioned awareness and no higher consciousness.

What gives the self pleasure will also give it displeasure. The gift of joy emanating from the soul is from a different dimension and is beyond change.

Emotions relate to personal consciousness and they stabilise when reference is made to higher intelligence and consciousness. Anger occurs when an outer event clashes with one's expectations and values. Fear relates to preservation, safety and the unknown. Surprise is the response to one's inability to relate to an outer situation that does not fit into the existing pattern of one's knowledge and expectation. Distress arises when conflicting forces cannot be resolved and are internalised. Disgust is the expressed attempt to disconnect from an unsatisfactory outer situation. All these emotions could have a positive effect on one's spiritual growth if one were to refer to higher consciousness. A loving heart would not consider these emotions to be negative. The emotion of joy is, however, the result of personal consciousness being re-energised by pure consciousness. This is why we may say on such occasions that a heart has 'opened'.

Every cry announces distress, anger, fear and other objections of the self. Every joy is a signal of a degree of unison between the self and soul.

The law of complementary opposites is inescapable at all times. The wise seeker will see ease within every difficulty. The loss of a job, for example, could mean a respite from an unsuitable work environment. Whenever faced with failure, difficulty or constriction, look with your heart's eye for the hidden opportunity and unexpected goodness or opening within those situations. The labels of success and failure mask other meanings and messages. Affliction is never too far from a blessing, neither is a blessing without any tarnish. Look for the good in what is considered bad and witness the seeds of potential badness within what is regarded as goodness. Reflect upon your misplaced expectations and wrong assessments. Witness the perfection of divine justice in every situation and try to live and act justly within human limitations. Faith in god means being secure in and certain of god's perfection and the human possibility of witnessing perfection within all situations.

When you experience constriction and need, do not pity the self; just do your best and then read the signs and meanings of the situation. Accept and know.

The spiritual path entails the disciplined avoidance of the self's lower egotistical tendencies, emotions and confusions. Grooming the self begins when one turns away from greed towards modesty, from anger to courage and wisdom, from lack of care to compassion, patience and justice. Every connection and relationship reveals an aspect of the inner state of your self. Consider every act as a dedication and devotion to the soul. Undertake outer activity or recreation that brings about a release of tension, relaxation and a feeling of well-being. Love the qualities that open up your heart and connect you with higher consciousness.

The more you say 'no' to the self or the ego, the more your heart may say 'yes' to you.

You can cultivate your imaginative faculty and insights faster by leaving behind previous habits, emotions, expectations, judgements and other mindsets which will restrict inner growth and evolvement. Break them before they stunt your spiritual growth. Resistance to change in life is often due to the self seeking constancy and stability, whereas the self's own nature is contrary to that; restless and unstable. Every human being is motivated by self-interest, which is egocentric to start with but as it grows in wisdom and matures becomes more heart and soul oriented interest. The gross can lead to the subtle and the low to the high.

Genuine real fun begins when the self views existence through the joyful eye of the soul.

Seeking ancestral roots is an aspect of our search for the original source of life. The self is designed to seek its soul. It is only through unity of consciousness that one attains wholesomeness. The exact path of personal spiritual growth differs from person to person and does not follow a predictable time scale. The seeker needs to be determined, focused and attentive, yet inwardly relaxed and trusting in the best outcome. Be outwardly responsible for intention and conduct and you will realise increasing inner awareness and connection to heart.

The higher rational mind connects at heart with the soul and its lights of insight, inspiration and divine consciousness.

As the self evolves spiritually, one experiences how every good and bad meet, and vices and virtues are inseparable. This is how the self transcends the mind and its limitations to arrive at the heart and the domain of the boundless. Greed for worldly possessions is a vice but its root is for the self's greed for knowledge and contentment. Anger against others is a vice but against the ego and ignorance is a virtue. Turning the cheek is for one's own self-effacement, whereas defending a good cause can be for the sake of others, when guided by wisdom and compassion.

The soul is like a movie screen that allows the changing images and shadows of the self to be cast upon it – good or bad.

Wean the self from the destructive addictions of outer excess, such as food, alcohol and irresponsible sexuality; hook it to the passion for inner calm and spiritual insight. Whenever you notice a vice, see the virtue next to it and connect with it. Turn away from your shadow and you face light. Reject meanness and what you face is generosity. Turn away from fear and you are on the highway of courage.

The duality within us reflects in outer dualities. Unify inwardly and you will experience unity at all levels.

The values of kindness, goodness, peace, tranquillity, harmony and happiness are as good as their duration or sustainability. We love long-lasting goodness. The soul knows only goodness, as it depicts divine perfections. The self longs for that state and can only live it when it is in unison with the soul. The reward of the surrender of the self to the soul is sublime ease and contentment.

People are enemies of what they do not know. Prophets and messengers are carriers of divine light to other hearts. They are naturally often denied and betrayed by rebellious selves near them.

This world contains samples of all creations and states, seen and unseen, including paradise and hell. Human life is a process of learning through acceptance and rejection. To activate and access your heart, you need to reduce outer worldly concerns. To understand fully the greatness, power and perfection of the present moment, you need to cleanse the mind from its past or future fears. Only then can you live now. To be more in heaven you need to be less worldly. To live the moment fully, you must go beyond space-time.

Outer stimuli and excitements need to be balanced with inner security and stillness.

Worldly pursuits are never fully satisfiable; like a fire, they demand more fuel the more they have been given. Obsession with one's work is a clear sign of desire for the fruit which may result from that work. Most people work for a so-called livelihood in an occupation not fully suited for their temperament. Many commercial activities are simply ways of making money with little or even negative human values in them.

When you allow the self to enter this treacherous alluring desert, it cannot easily find a way out and return to a balanced way of living. In this case there is no map, road or direction — just loss.

Obsessive concern with worldly work is a sign of deafness to the souls' call to connect head and heart. This call is more urgent than all other concerns.

The stricter and clearer the boundaries you place upon the self, the quicker is the growth in consciousness and inner guidance. To be free implies being able to access the zone of soul consciousness, which is connected to divine consciousness beyond space-time. This is the meaning behind the 'death' of desires and expectations: the more you turn away from worldly connections, the more you enhance your joyful inner stations.

The greater outer self restrictions the easier will be inner expansion.

What is bounded, restricted and delineated is complementary to the boundless and limitless. Infinity is rooted in the tiny entity of an electron or photon. To restrict the self is the first step towards the open horizons of the soul. Many spiritual practices and religions establish laws and boundaries without a clear outer logic or reason, for spiritual logic is totally different to the worldly version. Here you go against the self and its desire where normally you simply try to please the self without reliable satisfaction.

For spiritual progress we need to apply the opposite logic to that used in worldly growth.

Remembrance of death reminds one of how urgent the surrender of self to soul is. When somebody dies, the mourners will experience sorrow and loss but at the same time feel a breeze of mercy in the reminder of the temporary nature of this life. This is why we are encouraged to visit cemeteries and remember death. Die into your nothingness and you will live by the light of the eternal soul. Remembrance of death does not contradict the virtue of tenacity and persistence in outer activity. It actually complements it and brings grace to all worldly endeavours.

Remembrance of death may bring sadness to an ordinary person but brings a sense or urgency for the spiritual seeker. The sage cries when someone is born and laughs when someone has died.

A teacher, guide or role model is most helpful for spiritual progress. The qualified teacher is free from needing approval or disapproval. The student may be dependent upon the teacher but the teacher is free of from the views and evaluations of his student. Your company may be appreciated and enjoyed by the teacher but when you are absent it is not missed. The self of a real teacher will not be inflated by flattery; neither will self-worth be diminished by lack of gratitude or acknowledgement. Proper courtesy, however, is essential for the student's sake. If you love the teacher and not the teachings it is like wishing for light without a lamp or the sun. If you love the teacher *and* the teachings then you will benefit from all lights, suns, moons and stars. You are on the way to discovering the sacred light in your heart. With the help of an enlightened being this can happen when the wick is clean (pure heart) and there is protection from interfering worldly winds and the natural sabotages of a confused mind or ego.

The need for a spiritual teacher is like the need of a novice sailor for an experienced skipper or navigator. An accident near the shore is not fatal but to capsize in the middle of the ocean can be fatal.

Unless self-esteem, image and other egocentric tendencies are replaced with generosity and selfless acts, suffering and disappointment will prevail. Challenge your dark shadows and leave them behind. Reflect upon and read your present situation without emotional veils or prejudice. Remember that most actions are intended to bring about a reward, as evaluated by the self at the time. The question is whether the action was for the higher or lower self. Do not ever feel sorry for the self and always blame it. Never blame others, even if someone encourages you to do so. Acknowledge your failures, then empty your heart and mind of blame, anger, regret or disappointment. Then catch a glimpse of perfection in what you considered imperfect!

There can be no good without the seed of badness within it, no badness without some goodness within it. The only absolute good is divine goodness.

Acknowledge the self's earthly attachments, then leave them behind for the thrills of the soul's delights. Liberate yourself from your self; let your heart and soul guide you. Remember that how you see the outer world is a true mirror reflection of your inner state. Acknowledge your mind, ego and self but don't let past memories or emotion chain you down. Turn to embrace your soul in the wedding chamber of the heart.

All thoughts and intentions will manifest outwardly to varying degrees and levels. Thus, be most watchful with your emotions, thoughts and actions. Be aware and more aware.

The self always imitates the soul: it desires to control and rule as it attempts to take on the authority of the soul, which is god's earthly steward and agent. Personal experience is considerably different when the self exerts its own will, or when it simply adopts the soul's will. In the first case there is much confusion, in the second case there is clarity and contentment. Invoking god is an attempt to bring into effect cosmic (or soul) empowerment, rather than the self, mind or ego.

You are stable when there are no contradictory aspects to your action. Unite head and heart and act as one authentic person. Let the heart lead.

Do your best with what you are good at and your heart will reveal to you what is excellence in other endeavours. Do not be impatient with delays in reaping the fruits of your actions. When you are out of balance, or disturbed in any way, postpone decisions. Most regrettable events occur when one is in a rush and the heart is not referred to. Always acknowledge and pay attention to the small issues and then look for the bigger picture and fit the smaller one within the larger framework. Then look at the one light behind all the pictures. Do what is wise, sustainable and just, irrespective of short term self interest. By serving others, the self moves away from the futility of selfishness and mental traps.

If a fertile earth is not planted with desirable plants, it will fill up with all kinds of invasive weeds.

Cultivate the habit of gratitude and inner contentment. Always acknowledge the goodness in a situation and other people's helpfulness. Cultivate self accountability and express shame and regrets whenever the self causes offence or transgresses boundaries. If you connect head and heart, the different levels of consciousness will be synchronised and come together in harmony. Ultimate salvation and spiritual awakening occurs due to unity of consciousness.

What you dislike may be your remedy, while what you like could be your poison and misfortune. Choose whatever elevates you spiritually.

Seeking knowledge is like prospecting for precious stones. Once you are near your target, you need to dig with suitable equipment, then select the stones, take them out for a final cut and polish. Your equipment is a focused mind, determined disciplined action, then discernment and differentiation and ultimately the use of this experience and knowledge in future thoughts and actions. Action produces knowledge and wisdom which are the seeds of transformation.

Think of what is absent and you will experience absence. Live with presence and absence will vanish.

Mindfulness, groomed and evolved, will lead to mindlessness and heart-fullness. A clear mind is necessary but insufficient, for it is the heart that knows the truth. If the self is to read the heart, it first needs to be distracted from the shadows of self interest, so as to connect with the heart. You can only taste honey after spitting out the bitter aloe in your mouth. The immortal soul beams its numerous lights on the entire human kingdom, with its complex physiology and cosmology. The soul contains the foundations of everything that is understandable; its role is fulfilled when the self is aligned with it. When this harmony between the self, body, mind, heart and soul is established, the map of human composition is lived efficiently and the seeker reaches the intended destiny of witnessing perfection joyfully.

Reading the map with urgent attention and then following its codes of transformation will bring about arrival at the perfect destination.

7.3. KNOWLEDGE AND ACTION

Appropriate outer actions follow relevant intention and knowledge. When higher consciousness is brought into the equation, the outcome becomes most effective.

The human being is like a living astrolabe that can read, feed back and respond to data and events. An accurate instrument needs constant physical care and maintenance. Therefore the information that is fed into it must be reliable and relevant. Then one needs to read the output correctly and according to relevant calibration. The last and most important point is to act and respond to the instrument's reading. The combination of these factors produces healthy living, poised for increased knowledge and new and efficient action.

A healthy body, a clear mind and sharp intellect are preludes to accessing the heart.

Everything in creation relates to other creations, often imperceptibly. A painter uses colour combinations to highlight harmony; a musician relates to sounds; a physician links cause and effect. Universal connectedness is what holds creation together but we often only look for the relevant or useful relationship within perceptible space and time. At a practical level of seeking harmony in relationships, relevance and context are key factors. This implies specific knowledge, as well as higher consciousness applied to the situation at hand. Look at what is in front of you as well as on the horizon.

To know is to reproduce in the mind the pattern of what is already known to the soul.

The quest for knowledge in this life never ends, for every knowledge is part of a vast domain of energy fields and patterns dormant within the soul's consciousness. On a journey you require some understanding of the basic condition of the terrain, its geography, topography and overall environment. It is part of a person's maturity to know the basic characteristics (outer and inner) of relevant entities and factors in life's landscape. 'Actions' unpack knowledge and insights by personally experiencing, connecting and sensing the meaning of that aspect of knowledge and wisdom. When knowledge is accompanied by an action it does alter physical situations and entities. Thus, when knowledge changes so do things. Action and knowledge are never separate.

Action is like unpacking a parcel whose inner content is knowledge and meaning. The more deliberate and thoughtful an action is, the more useful and revealing the content will be.

Knowledge and action complement each other at several levels: personal and societal, inward and outward, tangible conduct and unseen intention, conscious and unconscious. Drawings and descriptions of a tree give you basic knowledge of what a tree is. Action is experiencing through the senses the different parts of the tree: touching, tasting, smelling and having a direct experience of the tree. During life on earth, most of our actions involve acquiring something or 'becoming', only a few are for 'being' or connecting for its own sake. The cybernetic relationship between outer action and inner knowledge continues like a spiral, with the base having the physical aspects of life; higher up there is meanings and knowledge. Actions activate primal patterns, which connect with personal consciousness, which in turn reveals knowledge dormant within the soul consciousness. Outer action removes the veils from inner knowledge, which was already there.

Outer action brings inner knowledge to the surface. Knowledge and action are two companion facets which are needed to reveal excellence.

In everyday life it is vital to make clear distinctions at all times between worldly, tangible and material operations on the one hand and the domain of meaning and the subtle inner state. Worldly wisdom, plans and projects are different from heavenly or spiritual wisdom, which relate to truth and the higher levels of human consciousness. This is why hearts and minds cannot be easily won by outward plans and actions only, no matter how well intended these actions are. To combine heavenly and worldly wisdom is the goal of every intelligent person — who is in the first place a combination of the outer material world, as well as the subtle, multi-dimensional inner worlds, seen and unseen.

Fear can be one's worst enemy for its primal purpose is to urge the self to seek the soul – the fear of missing that boat.

Worldly projects and challenges are necessary to train and develop the self to achieve synchronicity and harmony with the heart. Caring for a project and focusing attention will teach the self the art of uniting the head and the heart, resulting in lasting ease and success. Excessive concern will be counterproductive and can cause failure. At the start, most of one's actions are carried out with little knowledge and this results in numerous mistakes. Experience brings hesitancy, reflection, patience and then appropriate action. Fear is a great friend when it produces reflection and patience, but an enemy when it causes mental blocks and paralysis.

Caution and uncertainty with regards to outer actions are far better than over confidence, inattention and vanity.

Personal consciousness is swaddled in ignorance that is slowly removed, lifted through growth, need, desire and action. Honest ignorance and uncertainty can lead to clarity and decisiveness. Ambition is a primal force that drives the self initially towards outer achievement and later on towards its ultimate fulfilment of enlightenment. Early in life, much of this force appears as actions with little knowledge. Wisdom implies less action and much knowledge. Optimum action utilises smooth natural power and little force. When a person rides with confidence and contentment upon the tide of destiny, work becomes effortless. Perfect action is always effortless. Action then becomes like the small quantity of yeast in a loaf of bread and knowledge is like the flour.

Every living creation follows, with ease, what it had been created for. In the case of a mature human being the self (mind) and ego cause difficulties which indicate the need to go past them.

The common person is preoccupied with the success and failure of an action, whereas the awakened being acts efficiently and is absorbed with perfection, irrespective of the outer outcome of the project. When self and soul are in unison numerous new knowledges become apparent. When the moon faces the sun fully it reflects maximum light. So does the self when it acts out with higher qualities of the soul, compassion, generosity, patience and so on.

Windows of creativity and insight open when you are relaxed and not anxious about results. Only then you can travel safely into the unchartered territories of the intangible world of inner delights.

Action alone cannot bring about transformation, yet it is by wrong and egotistical action that the self is misled further and 'deformed'. Thus, appropriate and selfless actions are necessary but insufficient. Occasionally they are a stumbling block if the self takes delight in the reputation of its 'good deeds', 'piety' and virtues. Self-righteousness is a major pitfall for all 'good' people. The combination of selfless action and a passion for truth can bring about transformation of the self, by propelling it to the abode of the illumined soul.

When you concern yourself with what does not concern you, you will miss giving attention to what should concern you and is important for your evolvement.

Human consciousness needs movement and change for growth and expansion, whilst spiritual evolvement relates to higher consciousness and insights beyond worldly logic and reason. Most outer desires and actions distract the self from caring for the heart and connecting to it. Initially the self acts with little experience or knowledge but soon relevant signs begin to guide one's action towards appropriate goals. The timing of the action, its quality, quantity, order and priorities are critical to any project or endeavour in life. Knowledge and action interact in subtle ways, so that the more one knows, the more intuitive one's moves become. To reach a physical destination is much easier than to reach a deep meaning. Much rarer is appropriate guidance to self-realisation and freedom from self illusions beyond mental barriers and pitfalls.

Animals mostly follow instincts – the gross always precedes the subtle. We need to follow the reasoning of intellect and until we enter the zone of inspiration and intuition.

The more you experience outer agitation and turmoil, the more you need to bring the restless self to rest at heart. Worldly needs and the sufferings from physical deprivation stimulate the drive towards material gains and wealth. Mental needs drive the self towards intellectual fulfilment. The latent inner spiritual thirst drives the self to unite with the soul. All these needs need to be addressed during human growth. Always expect that right answers, openings or inspirations will come to you at the appropriate time. We can only attempt small perfect acts. The rest is given to us by the soul, the personal godhead residing within.

Acknowledge the past without sorrow or regret. Live in the present moment fully and expect the best of the future. Trust in god's unconditional love and generosity. Your soul confirms his covenant.

Be aware and alert with high anticipation and patience. See problems as the means by which the soul bestows its gift of answers. Before the self asks the answer it is there waiting to be plucked. The power of rationality and reason relate to the outer world of duality in order to harness and guide the self. It is natural for the self to be restless and insecure. The feeling of not getting anywhere, or wasting time or opportunity, is a natural reminder for the self to reach the heart and rest in the unifying embrace of the soul. The self loves to exercise outer power and control, whilst it lacks any sustainable independent power. The seeker enjoys situations in which the self is powerless and exhausted. Victory in defeat.

According to your inner state the outer enterprise or project will call you to it.

Recalling your past problems and fears will make you realise the fallacy and transient nature of what you had considered important, urgent, agreeable or disastrous at that time. Yet, essentially you are the same person who still describes the ever-changing self as 'myself'. Remember that the soul is ever-constant but the self is ever-evolving. Essentially, you are a soul covered by the ever-changing shadows of the self, an eternal perfect true light activating a shadow in the worldly box of space-time.

The oldest and deepest memory relates to that point where there was no memory, only primal knowledge and god's design within the soul. Everything in time has its origin in non-time.

Only mundane and tangible desires and needs can be defined and pursued by action. Higher and sublime purposes, such as lasting joy, occur spontaneously as a result of knowledge and light emitted by the unison of self and soul. To forgive, be generous and always accept the truth, as it manifests, is to humble the self and offer it in submission to the soul. When there is no shadow, there is only light.

After years of struggle along the path a self-pitying voice complained that for too many years it had been knocking on the door of enlightenment with no results. The voice of truth answered that the knocking was heard but from inside the sacred house. Truth is always in our heart yet we search outside.

The self is a living parody of the soul. It is evolving in the world of interchanging dualities, yet desires the constancy of unity. The intrinsic nature of the self is change and inconsistency, thus it longs for timeless and reliable truth. It is living in its own personal war zone, yet longing for peace. When the self is transformed by the realisation that it has no independence from its soul, pure consciousness prevails over personal consciousness and puts an end to apparent dualities, flooding the heart with the light of unity. Then all twos are acknowledged but only as indicators of their root in one.

Our world of dualities and multiplicities is the outer skin of the world of eternal unity.

Consciousness generates willpower with a hierarchy. Following one's will at any time will result in some visible outcome, which varies considerably in acceptability or desirability according to how appropriate that will is and its context. Personal consciousness derives from soul consciousness, which is a beam of the supreme cosmic consciousness, which is an attribute of god whose essence is beyond all possible definitions, qualities and attributes. Each of these powers contain special patterns of willpower at different levels. The supreme consciousness prevails over all and the soul's will supersedes that of the self. Thus, it is vital for one to ponder upon divine will before exercising self will arbitrarily and without higher reference.

When the self is in unison with the soul, then personal will is subservient to the soul which reflects divine light, power and will.

The question of how to speed up enlightenment arises from the lack of understanding the nature of the two different realms and their respective maps and highway codes. The subtle and inner heavenly kingdom requires absence from worldly pursuit and following soul consciousness, whereas the outer kingdom requires determination, strong will power and struggle. Balancing the naturally interacting inward and outward aspects is needed to bring about harmony, balance and heightened awareness in one's life. This is the starting ground to perfecting the relationship between action and knowledge. The soul only sees perfection at all times. The self tries to unfold perfection through action. With spiritual wisdom, the self will witness perfections through the soul's lens. At the end, as in the beginning, there is only the ever perfect divine cosmic soul, the source of all knowledge and action and the creation's desire for ever-lasting perfection. God is beyond it all and yet all is covered by his essence.

Acting correctly implies coming one step closer towards harmony, peace and perfection. The best of all actions is submitting the self to the soul, then experiencing the world through the unifying lens of the soul within wholesome heart.

7.4. INTEGRAL ALCHEMY

In essence you are a sacred soul miraculously giving life to a self with body, mind, senses and other countless organs. Heavenly alchemy occurs when self and soul embrace at heart.

Outer technology increases personal skills, ability, competence and power. Driving a car is a magical extension of our normal walking speed. A quick-fix prescription drug can override a chest pain immediately but may have little lasting effect in curing the illness itself. All these outer aids help to increase human power with costs or side-effects not simple to calculate. Nevertheless, the self is always looking for props and aids for increases in efficiency and ease. The self is always looking for ways to get close to the state of the soul and its constant perfection and contentment.

The self is in constant change and evolvement and only experiences freedom from confusion after its alignment with its soul.

The highest human achievement is synchronising outer rationality with inner intuition and insights. It requires reading the map of human creation, understanding it, and following it carefully and attentively until the reader and that which is being read unify. When the self and soul are in harmony and unison, the person is potentially in an optimum state of fulfilment and authenticity. This alchemical fusion enables personal conditioned consciousness to unite with soul consciousness. There is a big difference between reacting to outside stimuli and challenges, and acting upon clear direction with continuous self correcting adjustment.

When there is no way out, look for the way in. Instead of climbing out, slide into your heart. Therein lies the essence of all.

Spiritual evolvement brings about synchronicity between the microcosm and macrocosm, between the outer and inner, meaning and form, tangible earthly and intangible heavenly. A new state of unity shines through connections and relationships far subtler than normal understanding. Good and bad, easy and difficult, ugly and beautiful, all meet in this new field of oneness. This new state reconciles and overrides all others aspects of duality, individuality and whatever is subject to change and relativity. This state occurs when the self has lost itself to its soul and is thereby transformed; like a lump of coal next to a fire it takes on the new glow and loses its old brittle black characteristics and identity. The ancient alchemist's art was to transmute the base lead of the self into the golden soul through practical spiritual disciplines, thereby spiritualising matter and material-ising spirit — a perfect blending of lights.

Human consciousness needs to experience the strife of duality in order to rise through choice and knowledge back to the bliss of unity.

The self's love for wealth had produced historically a culture of false alchemy and a crude attempt by primitive chemists to change lead into gold. The real alchemist is concerned with the process of self-purification and the self's unison with the soul and supreme light. The word 'alchemy' is derived from medieval Latin *alkimia* – which was borrowed from Arabic *kimiya*, implying black earth – and the Greek *chyma*, which means 'smelting' or 'casting of metal'. The implication is to melt the self, then recast it in its original spiritual format. By taking out all personal impurity and then burning the remaining base metal into ashes, the outcome will be the resurrection of the soul. The alchemical process attempts to volatise solids, solidify the volatile and partake actively with divine consciousness. The 'philosopher's stone', which is supposed to turn base metals into gold or silver, represents the catalytic presence of the cosmic soul and supreme consciousness.

The metal lead represents the heavy and unstable conditions of the self; gold is congealed light. The transformation of human lead into its golden soul is the return to universal beingness.

In the same way that we learn outer skills, the serious seeker of truth needs to learn and apply the inner rules of the spiritual journey. This requires mindlessness and total transcendence from all that is tangible and discernable. Whereas outer technology is worldly and based on reason and logic, inner technology is heavenly and has its own supra-logic. These two systems do not mix but meet within the human heart. These two domains are like the material outer world and the subatomic quantum world. When you are dealing with worldly matters, follow the path of outer discipline, excellence and efficiency. When it comes to heavenly (spiritual) matters, go against the self and its tendency – choose to oppose the self/ego to constrict and restrict the shadowy endless demands. Transformation transcends all discernable states and descriptions.

When you are less obsessed with your outer project and existential matters you experience a joy higher and more reliable than all worldly pleasures.

To go beyond one's identification with the self and its domains of body, mind and memories, one needs divine mercy, grace and the power of transformation. Clarity of direction, trust and a realistic agenda are all important for such progress but insufficient. When the sincere seeker is confronted by a problem, he needs to embrace it courageously with mind and heart and in time the answer will emerge from where it was not expected. A disappointing event already contains within it the keys for fresh and new appointment with renewed insight, knowledge and wisdom. Trust, act, be patient and surrender. All will be well as it always has been and will be.

What you consider a loss is the door to a new and better find, if you see with your heart's eye. Loss and gain are worldly exercises leading to eternal inner victory.

Be aware of all of your thoughts, for as long as there is a mind there will be ego and the instinct for self-preservation. As with everything else in creation, there are always at least two selves within us mirroring each other at any moment. The human self makes mistakes and the higher self (soul) is ever-forgiving. The self can make errors and is shown how to correct them by the compassionate loving soul. However, if it were not for the self and its imperfections, the soul's perfections could not be discerned. This is a milder version of the devil and god. The seeker renounces the self, whilst the enlightened one sees it as part of god's boundless mercy and perfect plan. How could there be a soul without a self within a person, or a light without a shadow on earth?

Spiritual transformation is no less a miracle than the transformation of a base metal to gold. Both are natural processes which show that the essence of all relative manifestation is absolute eternal light.

Live and act as though you are constantly being watched and recorded by an inner camera which misses none of your intentions, thoughts or actions. Whatever one does or thinks has its effect inwardly and outwardly, one way or another. You cannot retrieve what you have said or done; therefore, only say and do that which comes from your head and heart together and after reflection. Maintaining silence on regular bases is a great spiritual exercise. Today's negative thoughts or emotions are tomorrow's sickness. Whatever is within the self will reveal itself somehow. Be totally accountable and responsible for everything. Expect the best always and catch the perfect moment through your heart's presence and vision. Time is precious and yet endless when perfection is witnessed, worrisome and pressuring when worldly concerns dominate, worthless when the darkness of the ego overwhelms.

To learn and accept self boundaries and limits early on in life is often like having earned keys and openings to the boundless spiritual domains later on in life.

Do not look for faults and mistakes in others, for in truth there is no otherness which is independent, separate or far away from oneness. The lesson from a betrayed trust is not to stop trusting but to have compassion for the treacherous culprit and one's mistaken expectations. All souls are the same whereas selves are different in their restlessness and output as expressed in language or action. The self is least reliable (as a flickering shadow) whereas the soul is a true reference .The difficulty in human relationships is to know which 'shade' of the self you are relating to, the lowest self is at one end or the soul at the other.

Trust is based on truth, which is latent within the soul. The self desires outward trust which is relative, and then it realises that the source of all trust is the soul within.

Always blame the self for its lack of willingness to surrender to its soul. Be especially careful when other people admire or ennoble you. Know that the self is tricky and any self esteem will impede spiritual progress. The self must always be humbled, the soul honoured and the heart kept pure. When you are admired or acknowledged, neutralise this mistaken identity by redirecting this acknowledgement to the soul and its praiseworthy qualities. At best the self is a minor reflection of the good qualities and perfection of the soul, but its arrogance and vanity are major obstacles in its surrender to truth. Make sure you perform your duties. Your rights are always taken care of. By concentrating on what is not true, the truth will reveal itself. That is the secret depth behind the litany of 'no God but the (one) God'.

A spiritually evolved person is cautious of the pitfalls of self-deception, illusion and delusion and ascribes spiritual wisdom simply to unify in consciousness.

When you face difficulties, failures and the inability to change the world, then just change your mindset, attitude and recognise limitations. Do not allow fears and doubts to darken your heart. They can be dealt with by the intellect and then disposed and discarded. Tackle outer challenges with the rational self whilst protecting your heart from worldly poisons. Fears arise due to lack of presence in the moment and therefore anxiety about the future. Fear and hate are twin brothers who vanish with knowledge and love. View outer problems as insignificant and even irrelevant. Then look at them again simply as messages in need of meanings. Radical solutions are often found unexpectedly and at critical points. Be willing to leave your project or goal any time with no regret, sorrow, anger or disappointment. An anxiety is a cause for loss of energy and power.

To unify your role of 'becoming' and of actually of 'being', the self and soul need to be in unison and gathered at heart.

Always trust that you will experience the best outcome and witness that perfection by the grace of god and his encompassing mercy. This is transformative faith or trust. What appears as imperfect is veiled perfection behind misconceptions and lack of understanding of the situation. Everything in existence has occurred due to the perfect creator who has enveloped the universe with his supreme cosmic consciousness. Remain ordinary (as a person) whilst exploring the most extraordinary experience of life. Remember death and you will live every moment with intense vitality, gratitude and joy.

The stricter and clearer the boundaries you place upon the lower self, the greater your access to the heart's sanctuary and the soul's perfect presence and guidance.

The process of growth and evolvement of the self implies discrimination, knowledge and worldly wisdom, and the deeper meanings behind appearances. There is always another picture within the obvious one but you need to change your focus from the obvious image in order to discern the hidden one. Then there is still a deeper, inner essence. Ultimately you bask in the inner light of pure consciousness, where no picture has yet taken place. This is how the human alchemical process transforms all manifestations to exude their original divine unific perfection.

To be near your creator, you need to distance the self from the confusion of the world of duality and change. When the self merges with the soul, supreme consciousness extinguishes all shadows.

The self's fears of change and uncertainty are signs of its fragile rigidity and its egotistic entrapment. When a person faces a situation with courage and trust, the light of the heart and higher consciousness will dispel many dark shadows and ghosts. The nature of the soul and heart is to give; the self, mind and body's nature to take. Presence in the moment means spontaneously heightened consciousness at all levels. When the self is at peace and rests upon the heart then it is released from other tensions and is in communion with its soul consciousness. The soul's voice travels like light and encompasses both backward and forward directions in time. The more the self is reminded of worldly limitations and transience, the more it may be ready to give in to its soul. When the self surrenders unconditionally then it witnesses perfections at every moment. The purified heart never misleads and the soul will always lead to blissfulness by grace of the spiritual elixir. Then, the inexplicable realisation of absolute truth will bring to naught everything in existence except the original ever present light of the one.

The serious seeker is like someone climbing out of a deep well whose walls are collapsing. Once he sees the light above him, he does not get excited lest he cause the collapse of the entire loose wall. Hold your breath. Let the self die and you will realise the ever-living soul and that you were never inside a collapsing well; that was you somewhere in the distant past – or was it? Where? Shining gold cannot remember grey lead.

7.5. TRANSFORMATION

Acknowledge and respect creation with sincerity, then transcend it to the glorious presence of the essence of all of creation. Every created entity reflects an aspect of the original sacred reality.

The universe is held together by countless energy fields and subtle forces with patterns and designs woven by beams or strands of light with varying degrees of tangibility and subtlety. Numerous levels and dimensions resulting in our world of space-time. We aspire, within human limitations, to decode what is relevant to our lives, needs and drives. We also marvel at the mysteries of the universe above our galaxy and within the atom. We all seek durable contentment, stability and fulfilment in a world of uncertainties and change. Transformation to harmony and wholesomeness is the purpose of personal growth and spiritual evolvement.

Differentiate between brief outer success and permanent inner access (and lasting victory). One is causal and temporary; the other is constant and perfectly reliable.

Nature at all levels is loyally connected to its creational roots and source. We too endeavour to connect, balance and unify outer situations with our inner state. Spiritual success rests upon combining worldly understanding, knowledge and experience with the heart's wisdom, insights and intuition. Personal efficiency and progress in the world depends on a healthy mind and rationality, whereas spiritual evolvement implies transcending the mind to the light of the heart and soul. Transcendence is a state of outer (mental) thoughtlessness and inner illumination. When we experience perfection in meaning or form in the outer world of experiences, we simply catch a glimpse of the ever-present perfection of pure consciousness. This vision is beyond the limitations of the mind, its causal logic and personal consciousness.

See goodness in whatever has come to your life, even though the specific event displeased you. Then the spiritual habit of always seeing perfection will become your second (real) nature.

When the self attains synchronicity with soul consciousness, then outer realities, states and situations reveal their fundamental roots in the eternal light of truth as transmitted by the soul. All relative and space-time based occurrences lose their importance in the light of this perfect vision. The present moment in time is so intense and immense that it contains all past and future. This is where the absolute truth lies; everything else recedes from it and leads to it. Enlightenment implies total absorption and contentment with the eternal presence. Outer change in body and mind give us the illusion of progress and journey towards the higher. Although, in truth, the original light of lights was always there within our heart, outer effort is needed to transcend duality if we are to reach peace at heart.

The soul's mission in this world is to accomplish the task of unifying with its restless shadow – the self. This union signifies spiritual birth and enlightenment.

Duality is within all human thoughts and actions. The giver of something (care) is also the receiver (of praise). The loser (of status) is also the holder (sad memory). The occupier (of a job) is occupied (by concern for promotion). Everything in creation is both possessed (by soul) and is obsessed (by forms or values). The soul transmits pure consciousness to the self which in turn energises the body, mind and intellect by its personal or conditioned consciousness. Whatever emanates from the one cosmic essence appears with at least two facets, a beginning and an end. The essence or the truth behind all these realities is not subject to duality and is beyond all beginnings and ends. It belongs to another domain – god in heavens! Yet it is the cause of all that appears on earth.

The outer world and the viewer or experiencer of it mirror each other in space-time and thus reflect and reinforce each other's credibility and credentials.

Spiritual maturity is combining worldly wisdom with heavenly insights, intuitions and lights. To witness perfection and bring harmony between the outer and inner states is a perpetual drive, achievable to varying degrees by the serious seeker who strives along the path of transformation by divine grace. The wise person regards this world as a stage for awakening before the return to the abode of eternity. When the self submits to the ever-present soul it is transformed and transmuted like the alchemical change of base lead to stable gold. The act of personal transformation to the abode of unity echoes the original eternal state of god's oneness.

When raw information is internalised and transmitted as knowledge, its effect transforms the person's awareness to another level of consciousness.

For the self to see things for what they are, in essence it must look beyond the values of attraction and repulsion, good and bad. Personal consciousness and identity relates to flashes and frames in the mind and memory, like idols soliciting credence. When the map of reality is seen from all angles and levels then under-standing, compassion and contented submission to the moment and its perfection becomes a norm. Contentment, however, is not the same as complacency. It is when the person's intention, knowledge, action and attentions coincide harmoniously to bring about at every moment renewed and yet continuous inner joy and peaceful thrill. These are natural stages in the evolution of the self towards its intended divine destiny.

The evolved thinker takes cause and effect to their limits, then looks at the horizon beyond rationality and duality for unison.

Concern and anxiety about attaining enlightenment is a common distraction and barrier to one's spiritual progress. The self must give up everything in order to realise the perfect essence within everything. The self of an enlightened being is reconciled with personal powerlessness and attributes all power to the soul to which it has joyfully submitted. Proximity and unity at heart are keys to any lasting contentment. Even a child hugs the mother to get the feeling it desires. An embrace is the closest two bodies can be to feel as one. The self gains all by surrendering to the soul and loses all if it deludes itself with independence and freedom. When outer causalities and dualities are connected to their unifying essence personal consciousness is at unison with pure consciousness. This state is at the root of all transformations.

The soul is god's agent of revealingl his perfections to the self, so that his glories may be revealed and recognised within creation. God's oneness is veiled behind numerous creational dualities.

Until the time when witnessing perfection at all levels becomes a norm rather than the exception, one needs to learn to listen to and trust in the higher voice within the heart and discard other noises. Listen to your heart and ignore the clutter of the mind. When the self is happy to avoid worldly affairs and excitements, you are at the edge of the spiritual ocean of delights. Whoever is ready to leave this world cheerfully may be at the edge of the endless heavenly ocean of delights and bliss.

It is said that there are as many ways to god as there are human beings. Each being is on a trajectory that, when followed faithfully, can lead to its self realisation.

A grieving lover cried out to god, "O lord! After years of loneliness I have tasted the short-lived bliss of union with my beloved, who has just passed away. Show me your justice and mercy in this tragedy!" The heart's voice whispers back, "This love of yours was only a prelude for you to discover the everlasting soul-mate, residing here within me. You only lost a transitory earthly partner, whilst your ever-present beloved is in your heart beckoning you. When will you heed?" For those who face destiny cheerfully with trust and good expectations any loss or failure is a signal for new opening.

The heart is the transfer station between the heavenly domain of angels and light and the earthly world of energies and matter.

Only when we realise fully the sacredness of the soul are we able to pay due reverence to all life on earth. It is by constant reference to the soul that love and respect for life becomes natural to us. As the highest centre of consciousness, the human soul seems to be empowered to act as the divinely appointed earthly representative and steward. According to many revealed prophetic books this soul is god's gift to Adam and his descendents – the message that heaven and earth, all that is known and unknown, emanate from one god and this mystery lies within the heart and soul of human beings.

The spiritual seeker claims to be a body possessed by a soul. The awakened one knows that he is a soul veiled by self and body.

A spiritually transformed person recognizes that outer limitations and frustrations are well compensated by the constant awareness of the perfection and intimacy of the soul within. All limitations are insignificant compared to the gifts of pure consciousness and witnessing the wholeness of the wondrous universe. This discovery is the ultimate gift of god through knowledge and love of his desirable qualities. Every self is eager to find its own way to this discovery, for there are as many pathways to light as there are creations seeking that light.

The transformed being is never disappointed, nor does he see any situation other than perfect. Yet, he commends acts of kindness and relieves human suffering and ignorance.

When one has added to outer sight and thought insights and visions, god's perfect will and justice will be seen more clearly in worldly situations. When you have access to paradise within your heart, all worldly gardens lose their attraction: You have arrived at your intended destiny after passing through this temporary world. Now you realise that your abode is the timeless heavens, whilst reconciled with the passing shadows during your journey on this earth.

Enlightenment and self-realisation occur when the self is seen as a mere shadow in the effulgent light of the soul. When pure consciousness engulfs all personal consciousness at all times.

Whoever worships out of fear of hell may be saved from it; worshipping in order to reach paradise may also bring you to its sanctuary. But if you worship out of passionate adoration of god's ever-present perfection, the self will disappear in the ocean of ecstasy and the soul will 'resurrect' in the eternal lights of bliss. Enlightenment is the most mysterious spiritual issue; not even a great prophet can promise it to anyone. Information about it is abundant but transformation to that state is rare. Courtesy, patience and self effacement, generosity, humbleness are amongst the pre requisites.

The heavens may have many doors leading to god's presence, but the nearest door is in your heart and its key is your soul, which needs to be retrieved from the pouch of the self.

Your sickness is from you – but you do not perceive it.
Your remedy is within you – but you do not sense it.
You presume that you are a small entity – whereas within you is enfolded the entire universe.
You are indeed the evident book, by whose alphabet the hidden becomes manifest.
Therefore you have no need to look beyond yourself; what you seek is within you, if only you reflect

(Imam Ali ibn Abi Talib)

POSTSCRIPT

Surrender to the truth means witnessing perfection through the lens of the inner soul.

Duality is the root of every created entity. Our world of space-time is knitted by countless strands of complementary opposites, such as energy/matter, growth/decay, beauty/ugliness, good/bad, relative/absolute etc. All these diverse entities, attributes or beams of energy emanate and return to the one cosmic essence and source which encompasses the universal pool of discernable existence caught within the boundaries of space-time.

The pinnacle of all creation is the human being, who is composed of two complementary entities. One is the self, giving rise to the personality, mind, senses, emotions, intellect, self awareness and heart. These are energized by evolving, conditioned consciousness (consciousness is from the Latin root meaning knowledge). The other aspect of the human being is pure consciousness, not subject to the changing world of space-time and its limitations; it is based within the soul. Motivated by the forces of attraction and repulsion, the human quest ultimately culminates in the unity of these two levels of consciousness within the inner heart. It is by means of this unification that the meanings and roots of events and experiences are understood. Truth is an absolute reference regarding the eternal essence found within the purified heart where self and soul exist in contented union.

The peak of spiritual intelligence, human fulfilment or enlightenment, is the transformative outcome of the self discovering that every changing entity and reality in life is rooted in the one eternal source, ever present and true, not subject to change. This 'illumined' human insight unifies all levels of consciousness harmoniously and enables one to see perfection, irrespective of outer events or situations. Witnessing perfection and the joy of timeless presence occurs when one looks at the world of dualities and diversity through the lens of divine unity.

No worldly achievement or success will give a person lasting contentment at heart, unless harmony and inner synchronicity between self and soul is established. Most religions and ethical paths or prescriptions endeavour to transcend the ego and purify the heart so as to enable the inner lights of the soul to illumine and guide the self in its perpetual effort to achieve balance, peace and contentment.

Personal experience of the outer world of cause and effect and the drive to achieve balance or harmony within is in turn reflected in communities and societies. Just as there are levels of personal spiritual evolvement, so are there for peoples and nations. Most religions attempt to bring about higher knowledge and awareness of the ever-present supreme essence or god through personal and collective practices and the application of values to varying degrees of success.

Our present world is driven by science, commerce, technology and their globalisation. To bring about trans-cultural, global cohesion and understanding amongst the diverse cultures and religions of the world, we urgently need universal spiritual awakening. The outer techno-economic drives and dominance of the culture of consumerism require the stabilizing balance of inner personal spiritual awakening, beyond race, culture and religion. Human outer differences will fade in the light of discovering the sacredness and similarity of all human souls. When this higher awareness occurs, much of the present-day political, ideological, commercial and other conflict will be less rampant and pervasive. The so-called important global clashes and conflicts can only find a lasting solution in the spiritual realm. The outer clamour for worldly wealth and possessions can only be reduced when the personal joys of inner wealth begin to be mined.

Every person's journey in life begins with personal ambition, interests and actions aimed at outer success and fulfilment. Ultimately, the wise and intelligent thinker will realize that true happiness comes from a contented heart, which itself results from self-restraint, accountability and a passion for knowledge and truth. Thus, life begins with actions and desires and ideally culminates with contemplation, insights and delights in the ever-present perfections at every instant.

The soul contains all the desirable divine attributes for which the self yearns at all times — such as power, life, wealth, knowledge. It knows and reflects its supreme creator. The self is the shadow of the soul and tries to assume its higher qualities. The self loves security, power status and life while the soul is the source of life, honour and security. The human struggle is resolved by the discovery that these perfections are already within one's soul. This world is an arena for training the self to focus upon and submit to the perfect lights emitted from the soul. Metaphorically, Adam wanted to know cause and effect whilst he was in a twilight zone beyond time, space and the causalities of this world. The human soul had to 'descend' and interact with the ever-changing dualities so as to evolve in the realization that differences and divergence exist due to the unifying essence within them. Ascent and resurrection are the return of the self to the soul and experiencing that state which is already within the heart but veiled by space-time. The hereafter encompasses the 'here' and the purpose of life is to evolve and realise the ever-perfect moment here, now and after. There has been nothing other than the cascading divine light producing infinite varieties of shadows, all pointing to the ONE essence worthy of adoration and worship. To witness the light of the ONE is to witness only perfection.

BOOKS

O books

O is a symbol of the world, of oneness and unity. In different cultures it also means the "eye", symbolizing knowledge and insight, and in Old English it means "place of love or home". O books explores the many paths of understanding which different traditions have developed down the ages, particularly those today that express respect for the planet and all of life.

For more information on the full list of over 300 titles please visit our website
www.O-books.net

SOME RECENT O BOOKS

Son of Karbala
Shaykh Fadhlalla Haeri

A new dawn has appeared in spiritual travelogue with the publication of Son of Karbala. It deserves a place among the great spiritual odysses of our time, right next to Gurdjieff's Meetings with Remarkable Men, which it at once resembles and exceeds in its honesty and clarity. **Professor Bruce B. Lawrence**, Duke University, Durham NC
1905047517 240pp **£14.99 $29.95**

A Global Guide to Interfaith
Reflections From Around the World
Sandy Bharat

This amazing book gives a wonderful picture of the variety and excitement of this journey of discovery. **Rev Dr. Marcus Braybrooke**, President of the World Congress of Faiths
1905047975 336pp **£19.99 $34.95**

A Pagan Testament
The literary heritage of the world's oldest new religion
Brendan Myers

A remarkable resource for anyone following the Wicca/Pagan path. It gives an insight equally into wiccan philosophy, as well as history and practise. We highly recommend it. A useful book for the individual witch; but an essential book on any covens bookshelf. **Janet Farrar** and **Gavin Bone**, authors of *A Witches Bible, The Witches Goddess, Progressive Witchcraft*
9781846941290 384pp **£11.99 $24.95**